The Mysterious Play of Kālī

American Academy of Religion
Studies in Religion

Editor
Lawrence S. Cunningham

Number 56
TH MYSTERIOUS PLAY OF KĀLĪ

by
Carl Olson

THE MYSTERIOUS PLAY OF KĀLĪ
An Interpretive Study of Rāmakrishna

Carl Olson

Scholars Press
Atlanta, Georgia

THE MYSTERIOUS PLAY OF KĀLĪ

by
Carl Olson

Library of Congress Cataloging in Publication Data

Olson, Carl.
The mysterious play of Kālī : an interpretive study of Rāmakrishna / Carl Olson.
p. cm. -- (Studies in religion / American Academy of Religion; no. 56)
ISBN 1-55540-339-5 (alk. paper). -- ISBN 1-55540-340-9 (alk. paper; pbk.)
1. Ramakrishna, 1836-1886. I. Title. II. Series: AAR studies in religion ; no. 56.
BL1280.292.R36047 1989
294.5'55'0924--dc19 89-6093
CIP

Printed in the United States of America
on acid-free paper

This work is dedicated to Peggy,
my biggest critic, for her considerable labors and support
and to the memory of Louise.

CONTENTS

Preface ix

Introduction 1

Play (Līlā) 19

The Feminine Thread 33

Madness 47

Humor 69

Stranger 87

Visions 101

Conclusion 115

Bibliography 121

PREFACE

If you encountered someone who assumed the dress and demeanor of a woman yet held a misogynist attitude, would you not wonder about such a person? If you met someone who told a humorous story one moment and, then, acted like an insane person, would you not become intrigued by such a person? If you knew an adult male who acted like a child, played the role of a monkey, worshiped a fearsome goddess and his own penis, cried one moment and laughed the next, received visions, and talked to invisible beings, would you not consider such a person a mysterious puzzle in need of solving? Is it possible to unravel such a human puzzle and to understand such a person in a reasonably coherent manner?

These were some of the questions and problems raised after I read *The Gospel of Sri Rāmakrishna,* while I investigated another topic in Hinduism. Pausing to reflect on the fascinating religious figure of nineteenth-century Bengal depicted in this work, I was struck by two things: the message of Rāmakrishna for the current ecumenical age and especially by his behavior, which prompted me to reflect on parallels with religious figures from other cultures. While doing further research on Rāmakrishna, I discovered that most of the scholarly work on him was biographical in nature with little attempt to interpret the meaning of his behavior. Thus I decided to attempt to fill the gap and to discern the meaning of his often unusual actions.

Trying to come to grips with the hermeneutical mystery presented by Rāmakrishna was not an easy task. How was one to make sense of this strange figure and his relationship to Kālī, the Goddess of death and destruction? How was one to comprehend an individual who acted like a child, a woman, a madman, made jokes and told humorous stories, received visions of divine beings and mystified his contemporaries? A constant theme that manifested itself throughout his life was the concept of *līlā* (play), a purposeless, spontaneous and blissful activity. Thus the concept of *līlā* (play) was the hermeneutical key used to unlock the meaning of his relationship to Kālī, and other deities, his various religious experiments and his bizarre behavior.

When considering the message and behavior of Rāmakrishna, the most authentic source of information is *The Gospel of Sri Rāmakrishna* compiled by M (Mahendranāth Gupta) over a period of four years, while the Master was still alive. This work, however, presents a significant problem, if one takes seriously what Rāmakrishna said about Kālī and how he acted towards her. The term for a divine being in this work is often translated God. Since Rāmakrishna was an ardent devotee of Kālī throughout his life, I used the feminine form when referring to a divine being for the sake of accuracy unless a specific male deity is specified by the context.

Why did this text prefer to use the male reference to a divine being? In light of Swami Vivekānanda's advocacy of Advaita Vedānta philosophy, it appeared that he and members of the movement—The Rāmakrishna Math and Mission—became embarrassed by Rāmakrishna's devotion to Kālī and wanted to expunge her as much as possible and to correct their master by referring to ultimate reality in neutral or masculine rather than feminine terms. Although Rāmakrishna personally experienced male deities and the Vedāntic Brahman in his religious quest, devotion to Kālī was always central to his religiosity from early in his career until his death of throat cancer. Thus it is more faithful to the religious spirit and personal convictions of Rāmakrishna to refer to ultimate reality as feminine. In order to emphasize Kālī's significance to Rāmakrishna, I will consistently capitalize the term "Goddess" throughout this work.

Since it is easier to be more productive as a scholar in a stimulating academic environment, I want to thank the members of my department for their support, Provost Andy Ford for generously approving a typing grant and to President Daniel Sullivan for trying to make Allegheny College an even better place to work. I also want to thank Donald Vrabel of the library staff for obtaining numerous manuscripts for me. I want to thank Peggy, Holly and Kelly for their love, without which life would be rather bleak. Finally, I want to extend my sincere gratitude to Beth Reynders for her helpful editorial assistance.

This work would have included more extensive quotations from Rāmakrishna to support the positions taken in this study and to place his words within the context that they were uttered. Unfortunately, the Rāmakrishna-Vivekananda Center in New York City would not, however, grant me the permission to make extensive quotations. A committee at the center thought that this work does not depict Rāmakrishna in the best light. By granting me permission to quote from *The Gospel of Sri Rāmakrishna,* they thought that they would be endorsing the thesis of this work. This is, of course, absurd because I, like any scholar, accept all responsibility for what I have written, and do not seek any endorsement of my work from any religious body. When reading the following pages, the irony of this situation will become apparent to the reader: Rāmakrishna himself was receptive to many different ideas and tolerant of the beliefs of others. Apparently, we cannot make the same claim about his successors. Throughout the fruitless and frustrating endeavor to try to reason with my implacable and ardent censors, I appreciate the support that I received from the staff of Scholar's Press, especially Dennis Ford and Lawrence S. Cunningham.

Chapter I

INTRODUCTION

Taking some time off from the thoroughly enjoyable activity of severing human or demonic heads and drinking the blood gushing from the cleaved arteries of her victims, the Goddess Kālī tried another way to amuse herself and frolic with her creation. Pausing for a moment, during the nineteenth century, from her destructive activities, Kālī, as the divine *śakti* (energy), used her *yoga-māyā* (magical power) to play upon the earth. During this interlude, Kālī staged a real life drama adopting Rāmakrishna, a simple priest of the Dakshineswar temple north of Calcutta, to be her leading actor. Kālī not only directed this drama, but she also starred in the production herself as its leading lady. In other words, as part of her divine play *(līlā)*, Kālī composed the drama, directed it, starred in it and assumed the role of an impresario. What was she trying to accomplish by assuming all these roles? She played her many roles for no real purpose; it was all for fun, a simple diversion to amuse herself.

There are some interesting parallels between Kālī's production and *The Nāṭyaśāstra* attributed to Bhārata (ca. second century B. C. E. to second century C.E.). The latter text served as the archetypical treatise for all subsequent Indian dramaturgy and bound later theorists and composers of drama by its authority, even though some later authors did not adhere slavishly to it.[1] The playhouse of Kālī 's drama, for instance, was the temple at Dakshineswar, which represented the large type of playhouse intended for the gods, according to the classical dramaturigal text.[2] In contrast to the delicate type of production, the play of Kālī was the energetic type with gestures and dance movements by an actor impersonating a divine being.[3] The dancing, a needless activity, in the drama created beauty and was connected with love.[4] In Kālī's production it was the love of the leading actor, Rāmakrishna, for the director and leading lady, Kālī. Rāmakrishna was absorbed in the thought of his beloved Kālī, and he made amorous gestures and mimicked the sport *(līlā)* of his beloved, which was a manifestation of his affection for her, as advocated by Bhārata.[5]

---

[1]A Berriedale Keith, *The Sanskrit Drama in Its Origin, Development, Theory and Practice* (London: Oxford University Press, 1924; reprint 1970), pp. 294, 292.

[2]Manomohan Ghosh, trans., *The Nāṭyaśāstra* Vol. 1 (Calcutta: Granthalaya Private Limited, 1951; Second Ed., 1967): 2.11.

[3]Ibid., 14.55; 14.59.

[4]Ibid., 4.267; 4.313.

[5]Ibid., 24.19.

In the classical dramatic theory developed by Bhārata, the play gave relief to those afflicted with sorrow and grief.[6] The director also wanted to instruct the audience through entertainment, an artistic form of enjoyment culminating in complete relaxation . In a sense, the production of Kālī gave release from the tedium of ordinary existence and invited the audience to participate in the frolic and enjoy themselves.

Although not intending to convey conflict,[7] there were three prerequisites for a classical drama: story; hero; and *rasa* (flavor, mood, taste). According to these three elements, a drama took a definite shape without distinctions between tragedy, comedy or romance.[8] A drama critic would be challenged considerably to characterize the drama produced by Kālī as a tragedy, comedy or romance because each of these features can be discovered in her production. Although none of these types of drama tended to predominate in Kālī's production, the phenomena of play, as we shall witness throughout this work, was a thread that tied her mysterious play together.

Depending on the type of story and hero, one or more *rasas*, a final state of enjoyment or satisfaction, would be developed by a classical play. Without going into great detail of the classical aesthetic theory related to dramas, *rasa* (mood, sentiment) was the result of various *bhāvas* (feelings, emotions), which were reactions to the gestures or words of the actors. *Bhāvas* were derived from an external cause or determinant *(vibhāva)*, an immediate and involuntary reaction or consequent *(anubhāva)*, or a deliberate, voluntary, conscious reaction *(vyabhichāribhāva)* that took the form of a transitory feeling. The total effect of one's involuntary and voluntary reactions was called *sthāyibhāva* (dominant emotion) of which there are eight feelings (e.g., love, humor, horror, fear, etc.) that constitute *rasa*.[9] The drama directed by Kālī produced, as we shall see later, the emotions of love, mirth, fear and astonishment with love the predominant sentiment. Through the part played by Rāmakrishna, Kālī gave witnesses a taste *(rasa)* of her power and mystery and allowed viewers to relish her love. Kālī did not, however, intend to accomplish anything by means of her mysterious *līlā* (play); she was just a divinity trying to have some fun. By playing his role, Rāmakrishna became totally absorbed in the *līlā* (play) of Kālī to the extent of losing and forgetting himself.

TIME AND SETTING FOR PLAY *(LĪLĀ)*

In the nineteenth century, Calcutta, the capital of British India, was a place teeming with indigenous people and foreign British businessmen and administrators. Within this cosmopolitan center, indigenous and foreign ideas clashed. Many Westerners were critical of Indian religious beliefs and social practices,

---

[6] Ibid., 1.114.

[7] Keith, p. 279.

[8] Adya Rangacharya, *Introduction to Bharata's Nātya-Sāstra* (Bombay: Popular Prakashan, 1966), p. 52.

[9] *Nāṭayaśāstra,* 6.15-38.

whereas other Western intellectuals saw something of enduring value in the Indian tradition, a treasury of ancient religious and philosophical ideas worth studying. Numerous Indians were also critical of their inherited religious and social traditions, while others sought to preserve and defend their heritage. Some Indians were influenced by Western ideas and embraced them, while other more conservative Indians reacted negatively to Western influence. The intellectual ferment caused educational experiments and literary developments. The environs of Calcutta, the city of Kālī, in the nineteenth century was home for individuals of grand vision and myopic foresight. It was a location, in other words, for the best and worst of human beings. Some Westerners and Indians thought that they had much to learn from each other, whereas others from both sides thought that they had little to gain from the other party. But it was overall a place of great excitement and flux.

The inhabitants of Calcutta were exposed within a very short time span to over two thousand years of Western science, technology, philosophy and religion. Western technology was to spread gradually by means of engineering projects like canals, harbor works, bridges, roads, and finally railways. Medical science made its impact initially through Calcutta Medical College. The process of secularization was also introduced with the advent of British rule, and was given impetus with the development of communications, the growth of towns and cities, the institution of courts of law, increased mobility and the spread of education. Western educators, like Henry Vivian Louis Derozio at Hindu College between 1826 and 1831, exposed young Bengalis to ". . . John Locke on civil liberty and natural rights; Rousseau on the justification of a representative democracy; David Hume on the bankruptcy of metaphysics; Voltaire on the supremacy of reason, enlightenment, and good taste; Bentham on the reformation of the legal system to achieve the most happiness for the largest number; and last but hardly least, Tom Paine on liberty and the flowering of the human spirit."[10] The minds of Bengalis were also exposed to humanism and Unitarianism with its social gospel and rational form of religion. In addition to all these ideas was added the influence of Western science with its systematic method, apparent certainty about knowledge of the universe, utility of its knowledge gained for useful purposes, and optimism about its purpose and usefulness for the future improvement of humankind.

On the negative side of the intellectual ferment, there were the Christian missionaries critical of Indian civilization and its barbaric, benighted and degrading religions. Horrified by Hindu idolatry and widow immolation *(sati)* on the funeral pyres of their husbands, Evangelicals pressured the government, after securing abolition of *sati* in 1829 by Lord William Bentinck (Hindu reformers also fought, of course, for its abolition), to withdraw official patronage of certain Hindu temples and festivals.[11] Demonstrating little tolerance for thousands of

---

[10]David Kopf, *The Brahmo Samaj and the Shaping of the Modern Indian Mind* (Princeton: Princeton University Press, 1979), p. 43.

[11]Percival Spear, *A History of India* Vol. II (Middlesex: Penguin Books Ltd., 1965; reprint 1978), p. 130.

years of religious tradition, and convinced of their own cultural and religious superiority, Evangelical missionaries attempted to convert and civilize unfortunate Indians to the "true faith." This kind of cultural imperialism was not without an ironical twist as Kopf indicates:

> What the missionaries seemed to achieve, unwittingly for the most part, was not the conversion of Hindus into Christians but the conversion of 'heathens' into reformed Hindus. The challenge of orthodox Christianity in India stimulated the Hindu intelligentsia to rediscover the sources of their own religious tradition and to reform their religion according to their new image of the remote past.[12]

Thus Christian missionaries became agents for the perpetuation of Hinduism in its revivalistic form. European missionaries also made important positive contributions by establishing schools, orphanages, hospitals and making Indians more sensitive to social and religious reforms.

The inhabitants of Calcutta also witnessed various educational reforms. The Calcutta School Society, the School Book Society, and Hindu College were part of this movement. The latter was the sole European institution of higher learning in Asia offering a science curriculum of chemistry, mathematics, astronomy, mechanics, hydrostatics, optics, anatomy and medicine. Bengalis accepted the educational experiments without dissent because it was intended to promote indigenous change from within the culture.[13] Furthermore, Indian faculty members were employed at the College of Fort William, originally a training center for British civil servants wórking in India established by Governor-general Marquis Wellesley by the turn of the century. This institution also encouraged cultural exchanges between East and West, and was the first institutional library of Oriental books and manuscripts.[14] As part of the educational changes, Bengali newspapers were established that carried local and foreign news. Books and periodicals were published in native languages and English. And as early as 1816, Calcutta had a free public library for its residents.

Foreigners with forsight and an appreciation for Indian culture were to be found in Calcutta along with others lacking these qualities. Since 1784, Calcutta was the home of the Asiatic Society of Bengal founded by Warren Hastings. Along with the College of Fort William, the Asiatic Society promoted Orientalism by translating important texts, publishing dictionaries, doing historical research and promoting archeological investigations into India's past. Scholars like William Jones, H. H. Wilson, C. Wilkins and H. T. Colebrook made significant

---

[12]Kopf, p. 157.

[13]David Kopf, *British Orientalism and the Bengal Renaissance: The Dynamics of Indian Modernization 1773-1835* (Berkeley: University of California Press, 1969), p. 181.

[14]Ibid., p. 6.

contributions to preserving and promoting Indian culture. Finally, the Orientalist Movement was killed by Macaulayism.[15]

The nineteenth century was also a period of important Hindu reform movements. None was probably more significant than the Brāhmo Samāj founded in 1828 by remarkable Rām Mohan Roy (1772-1833). While employed by the East India Company, Roy learned English and absorbed a confidence in modern science and aspects of Christian ethics. He based Hinduism on reason, the chief criterion by which to judge religio-social institutions and practices as expressed in the Upaniṣads. Roy spoke out most forcefully on the miserable plight of Hindu women, condemning compulsory self-immolation *(sati)* of a widow on the funeral pyre of her husband, seclusion *(purdah)*, child marriage, lack of educational opportunities and denial of property rights. He found image worship to be irrational, and he rejected the doctrines of rebirth *(saṃsāra)* and *karma*. Roy also founded the first Bengali newspaper.

The Brāhmo Samāj (originally called the Brāhmo Sabhā) was a reformist movement that adopted a congregational style of worship similar to Unitarian services for its deistic type of theism that was also like Unitarianism. The movement was later lead by Debendranath Tagore (1817-1905), but there developed a split in the movement when more liberal men like Keshab Chandra Sen (1838-84) insisted that members abandon their sacred threads and hypocritical behavior in not totally adhering to the movement's rational religion and code of ethics. The liberals lead by Sen wanted to encourage the following agenda: intercaste marriage; to abolish child marriage; to use Bengali in their worship services rather than Sanskrit; that ministerial rank be based on merit and not caste; and that members fully adhere to the rational tenets of the religion in their public and private lives.[16] The eventual schism between the conservatives and liberals resulted in the creation in 1866 of the conservative Original Brāhmo Samāj and the new and more popular Brāhmo Samāj of India.

After Keshub Sen took his new movement in the direction of Vaishnavism modeled on Caitanya devotionalism with its music, street processions and *sankīrtana* (singing devotional hymns), this restless spirit encountered Rāmakrishna around March 1875. Sen was both intrigued and influenced by Rāmakrishna's mystical type of Śāktism, which was to become part of the ideology of Sen's movement. Over a period of time, Sen publicized in his writings the teachings of Rāmakrishna, which introduced Rāmakrishna to a wider audience then probably would have occurred without the publisher's assistance. After being influenced by Rāmakrishna, Keshub Sen lost his interest in active social reform and turned to meditation.[17] Some members of his movement were convinced that he had betrayed the objectives of social reform, and another schism occurred in 1878 when Sen blatantly disregarded the movement's opposition to child marriage by marrying his daughter to a young mahārāja. The seceders formed the Sādhāran (general) Brāhmo Samāj, whereas the Church of the New

---

[15]Ibid., pp. 217-252.
[16]Kopf, *The Brahmo Samaj*, p. 132.
[17]Ibid., p. 139.

Dispensation, an attempted synthesis of Hinduism, Islam and Christianity, was formed by Sen.

Unlike the leaders of the Brāhmo Samāj, Svāmi Dayānanda Sarasvatī (1824-83) expressed no criticism of image worship, caste, child marriage, seclusion, or the plight of widows. Instead of social reform, he was more interested in restoring Indian culture to its former dignity and countering the conversion of low caste Hindus to Islam and Christianity, although social problems and community service did become a concern of the later movement. The ancient, divinely revealed Vedas were his source of inspiration and guide. Applying a yogic influenced hermeneutic to the Vedas, Sarasvatī rejected polytheism in favor of a single supreme deity and any religious developments after the Vedas as superstition. In 1877, he founded the Arya Samāj in numerous cities and set loose a militant ideology.

In summary, these were some of the technological developments, philosophical and religious notions creating the intellectual and cultural flux in nineteenth century Calcutta. With reference to the topic of this work, what was especially interesting about the intellectual and cultural turmoil taking place around Calcutta was that it had no perceivable influence on Rāmakrishna, who seemed completely oblivious or, at least, unaffected by the cry of cultural reformers, the technological changes around Calcutta, and the course of history. It was as if Rāmakrishna created his own little kingdom, impervious to any outside influence. We know that he had personal contact with educated individuals and reformers like Keshub Sen. Why did the influx of new ideas, the call for social reform, and emerging technology not affect Rāmakrishna? From his religious world-view, these were profane happenings and were as ephemeral as deciduous leaves. Thus the various winds of change yielded no final meaning for Rāmakrishna and need not divert his commitment to the religious quest.

THE HUMAN PLAYER

Since the biographies of Rāmakrishna recount the various incidents of his life,[18] it does not appear completely necessary to relate all the details because many of them will become apparent in later chapters. Thus I will attempt to avoid being repetitious. It should also be noted that aspects of his life are embedded in myth and legend, and some parts are modeled on, for example, the childhood of Krishna and Caitanya, the latter being a religious reformer of sixteenth century Bengal. Thus my objective is not to discover the true historical Rāmakrishna, but to examine some of the highlights of his life in order to place

---

[18]For useful biographical sketches of Rāmakrishna's life, see the following works: F. Max Muller, *Rammohan to* Rāmakrishna (Calcutta: Susil Gupta (India) Ltd., 1952); F. Max Muller, *Ramakrishna His Life and Sayings* (Mayavati: Advaita Ashram, 1951); Romain Rolland, *The Life of Ramakrishna,* trans. E. F. Malcolm-Smith (Calcutta: Advaita Ashrama, 1979); Christopher Isherwood, *Ramakrishna and His Disciples* (New York: Simon and Schuster, 1965); *Life of Sri Ramakrishna* (Calcutta: Advaita Ashrama, 1977); Solange Lemaitre, *Ramakrishna and the Vitality of Hinduism,* trans. Charles Lam Markmann (New York: Funk & Wagnalls, 1969).

the later chapters of this work in their proper context and to view him through the eyes of his faithful followers.

The biographical sources inform us that his father, named Khudiram Chaṭṭopādhyāya, received a prophetic vision in a dream, while his wife, Chandra Devī, had a wakeful vision before an image of Śiva in which a light emanating from the icon of the god entered her body and rendered her unconscious. After this experience, Chandra Devī began to have frequent visions and to hear voices. On February 13, 1836, she gave birth to a boy named Gadādhar, a name of Vishnu, at an allegedly auspicious moment in Kamarpukur, a village in the Hooghly district of Calcutta. The official name of the child was Sāmbhu Chandra, and he was born into a pious, orthodox, Vaishnava, Brahmin family that was devoted to Rāma, an incarnation of Vishnu, as their primary deity and other deities like Śiva and Durgā. This birth story bears similarities to those of Krishna and Caitanya. The birth story implies a divine conception, but not with a virgin, because Chandra Devī had already given birth to an older son in 1805, a daughter in 1810, and would have five childern during her life.

Similar to the biographies of Krishna and Caitanya, Gadādhar committed childish pranks. A change seemed to occur, however, in his life after the death of his father in 1843 when the youth was seven years old. The young boy became more introspective and liked to spend time alone. Itinerant monks may have had an influence on the youth during this period of his life. Because of the profound impact of his father's death, Gadādhar appears to have drawn closer to his mother and other village women. His personality and spirituality were further shaped by the ecstatic spirituality that he inherited from his parents and other family members. Gadādhar's early life was also molded by Indian village life and its local school, which he attended in an erratic pattern from the ages of five to seventeen. While irregularly attending the village school, he learned to read and write Bengali and to understand Sanskrit, although he was unable to converse in the latter language. The normal subjects taught in school did not appear to excite his interest nor curiosity. His interest in religious matters is suggested by his ability to memorize large portions of epic literature. Besides his memory for religious literature, Gadādhar possessed some artistic ability given expression by his skill to paint and form small images of Hindu deities. His artistic talent was also expressed by his singing of religious songs and dramatic capability by which he was able to play the part of a *gopī* (cowherd girl) in public plays reenacting the adventures of Krishna. The social and religious milieu of an isolated Bengali village, his less than rigorous intellectual development due to irregular school attendance and profound interest in religious literature, and his own family background shaped Gadādhar's emotional and aesthetic sensibilities.

The most dramatic change in his life occurred when he joined his brother, who possibly became a substitute for Gadādhar's deceased father, as an assistant at the Dakshineswar temple dedicated to the goddess Kālī in 1852. Rāmkumār, the older brother of Rāmakrishna, was invited to become a priest of the Kālī temple where he served until his death. Rāmkumār was chosen for a favor that he rendered to Rani Rasmani, a pious, rich, lower caste widow. Rasmani had received a vision in a dream from Kālī instructing her to build the goddess a temple on the banks of the Ganges River. Because of the widow's low caste status, no orthodox Brahmin priest would officiate as her priest. After receiving a letter about her problem, Rāmkumār devised a solution: she should make a gift of the temple to a Brahmin and endow it with sufficient funds for its maintenance. That this solution was heretical did not seem to hinder the determined Rasmani from building her temple on twenty acres of land at Dakshineswar, a small village approximately four miles north of Calcutta. It also did not appear to bother Rāmkumār that an orthodox Brahmin priest would accept a position from a low caste patroness at a Śākta temple.

Eventually, Rāmakrishna at age sixteen and Hriday, a nephew of his to be dismissed much later for improprieties, were asked to assume duties in the temple by Mathura Mohan, Rani's son-in-law and manager of her business affairs. After a priest carelessly broke a leg of an image of Krishna, Rāmakrishna suggested that it be repaired and not replaced. As a reward for his simple solution, Rāmakrishna was promoted to temple priest, after having been initiated by a Calcutta Brahmin named Kenaram Bhattacharya. It was after his installation that Rāmakrishna's behavior became consistently strange, a phenomenon that will be discussed in subsequent chapters.

Concerned about her son's strange behavior and mental state, Chandra Devī thought that marriage would restore his mental stability. On the verge of despondency over finding a proper bride for her son, Rāmakrishna located a suitable girl in a vision in the village of Jayrambati, three miles north-west of his village of Kamarpukar. After Rāmakrishna's marriage to Sarāda Devī, who was only five years old at the time, the girl's uncle returned to his village with the youthful bride over a disagreement about some ornaments given to her. Leaving his child-bride behind, Rāmakrishna returned to his priestly duties, a spiritual odyssey, gathering disciples, worshiping, making pilgrimages, and teaching.

In M's (Mahendranāth Gupta) diary of his encounters with Rāmakrishna over approximately a four year period, he related that it amazed him to learn that Rāmakrishna read no books.[19] Since M was a teacher and college graduate, it seemed to amaze him that Rāmakrishna could be an effective teacher without much education. M also noted that Rāmakrishna's English vocabulary consisted of only several words.[20] Although Rāmakrishna was not an educated individual by contemporary standards, he possessed a vast knowledge of the Hindu religious tradition. His teachings were a unique blend of several diverse and not necessarily complementary elements. Nonetheless, his most important personal asset was his charisma, which enabled him to influence Keshub Sen, Swami Vivekānanda and many others. Vivekānanda felt very deeply about his master. After returning from his trip to America to speak at the World Parliament of Religions, Vivekānanda spoke to a crowd greeting his arrival in Calcutta and referred in his address to his profound affection for Rāmakrishna: "Brothers, you have touched another chord in my heart, the deepest of all, and that is the mention of my teacher, my master, my hero, my ideal, my God in life–Shri Rāmakrishna

[19]M, *The Gospel of Sri Ramakrishna,* trans. Swami Nikhilananda (New York: Ramakrishna-Vivekananda Center, 1973), p. 78.

[20]Ibid., p. 278.

Paramahamsa."[21] Although Rāmakrishna made a lasting impression on the life of Vivekānanda, their teachings did not coincide. The more intellectual and better educated student adhered to and advocated Advaita Vedānta philosophy, turning away from the emotional devotionalism directed toward Kālī by Rāmakrishna.[22]

In April of 1885, Rāmakrishna's throat became inflamed, and he had trouble swallowing food. At first, his condition was not considered serious. After a hemorrhage of the throat, doctors definitely diagnosed his illness as throat cancer. M said that Rāmakrishna had to be tended all night by his followers taking turns staying awake with their master.[23] On August 15, 1886, Rāmakrishna died a little over a year from the beginning of his fatal disease.

After Rāmakrishna's cremation, M reported that disciples collected his holy relics.[24] But even more significantly, M recalled that his followers worshiped him as a deity.[25] For many people, Rāmakrishna was a saint during his life. Because saints are not allowed to remain on the boundary between the categories of man and god in India, Rāmakrishna was deified and made into an *avatāra* (incarnation). O'Flaherty observes, "In this view, saints are *born* saints; they do not achieve sainthood or have sainthood thrust upon them. They are *revealed* as having been saints all along (or, rather, gods)."[26] From another perspective, it can be said that Rāmakrishna was such an extraordinary individual to his disciples that the only possible explanation for them was that he could only be an incarnation *(avatāra)*. How else could one possibly comprehend such a mysterious person?

The retrieval of Rāmakrishna's relics after his cremation and the worship rendered to him are the beginnings of a cult. In his study of contemporary pilgrimage in West Bengal, Morinis states that the Dakshineswar temple is a popular place of destination for pilgrims. This is due not only to the renown of the saint, but also because of the five pipal trees forming the sacred *panchavati*.[27] This small cult outside of Calcutta would develop into a worldwide movement under the leadership of Vivekānanda.[28] But what kind of a movement was it?

---

[21] Swami Vivekananda, *The Complete Works of Swami Vivekananda*, 8 Vols. (Calcutta: Advaita Ashrama, 1970, Tenth Ed.), 3:312.

[22] Freda Matchett shows significant differences between Rāmakrishna's teachings and Vivekānanda in "The Teaching of Rāmakrishna in Religion to the Hindu Tradition and as Interpreted by Vivekānanda," *Religion* 11, (1981): 171-184.

[23] M, p. 955.

[24] Ibid., p. 977.

[25] Ibid., p. 978.

[26] Wendy Doniger O'Flaherty, *Women, Androgynes and Other Mythical Beasts* (Chicago and London: University of Chicago Press, 1980), p. 68.

[27] E. Alan Morinis, *Pilgrimage in the Hindu Tradition: A Case Study of West Bengal* (Delhi: Oxford University Press, 1984), pp. 18, 20.

[28] For recent historical surveys and interpretative studies of the movement, see the following: Cyrus R. Pangborn, "The Rāmakrishna Math and Mission: A Case Study of a Revitalization Movement," in *Hinduism: New Essays in the History of Religions*, ed. Bardwell L. Smith (Leiden: E. J. Brill, 1976; reprint 1982), pp. 98-119; George M. Williams, "The Ramakrishna Movement: A Study in Religious

When Rāmakrishna was alive and disciples gathered around him to listen to his teaching and perform *sankīrtana* (devotional singing) with him, there developed spontaneous communitas, possessing an immediate, concrete, non-institutionalized, and non-abstract nature.[29] Communitas, a unique modality of social relationship, can emerge at the edges of structure or beneath it. In the former instance, it represents marginality and in the latter it denotes inferiority. Spontaneous communitas is, however, only a temporary phase because it gives way to something more permanent. This was historically the case with the emergence of The Rāmakrishna Math and Mission.

Among the followers of Rāmakrishna, the most famous figure was Narendranāth Dutt (1863-1902) because of his role as an organizer and founder of the Rāmakrishna Math and Mission.[30] Born into a wealthy Bengali family that was *kayastha* by caste, Narendranāth graduated from college in 1884, during which time he was a member of the Brāhmo Samāj and supported its social reform programs, and was expected to follow the profession of his father, who was a prosperous lawyer in the Calcutta High Court. After the sudden demise of his father, he and his family struggled financially. In 1881, he switched his allegiance from the Brāhmo Samāj to the Adi Samaj led by Keshab Chandra Sen. In November of the same year, Narendranāth met Rāmakrishna for the first time, and was embarrassed when the saint identified him as Nara, the sage incarnation of Nārāyana.[31] Narendranāth lost sensory awareness of his body when Rāmakrishna touched him at another encounter in late December of 1881. These intermittent contacts with Rāmakrishna continued over a four year period until they became regular visits. Narendranāth did not share the devotional religious persuasion of Rāmakrishna because of his own convictions about the formless nature of ultimate reality and the necessity of social reform, although on June 13, 1885 Narendranāth experienced Kālī as a living reality with the assistance of Rāmakrishna. Even though Narendranāth was never initiated by Rāmakrishna, he did receive an appointment to guide the Master's pupils and maintain unity within the group.

Change," in *Religion in Modern India*, ed. Robert D. Baird (New Delhi: Manohar Publications, 1981), pp. 55-79; Harold W. French, *The Swan's Wide Waters: Ramakrishna and Western Culture* (Port Washington, NY: Kennikat Press, 1974).

[29]Victor W. Turner, *The Ritual Process: Structure and Anti-Structure* (Chicago: Aldine Publishing Company, 1969), pp. 125-165.

[30]For biographical material on Vivekānanda, I have relied on the following works: Swami Nikhilananda, *Vivekananda, A Biography*, Fourth Edition (Calcutta: Advaita Ashrama, 1982); George M. Williams, *The Quest for Meaning of Svami Vivekananda* (Chico, CA: New Horizons Press, 1974); George M. Williams, "Svami Vivekananda: Archetypal Hero and Doubting Saint?," in *Religion in Modern India*, ed. Robert D. Baird (New Delhi: Manohar Publications, 1981), pp. 197-226; French, *The Swan's Wide Waters*.

[31]Swami Saradananda, *Sri Ramakrishna The Great Master* 2 Vols., trans., Swami Jagadananda (Madras: Sri Ramakrishna Math, 1952; reprint ed., 1978, 1979), II: 825.

Narendranāth fulfilled his responsibilities for several years, but he left the fledgling group in 1890 and went on a pilgrimage of India to struggle with his doubts and to develop his own philosophical position. He eventually developed a position that combined the devotionalism of Rāmakrishna, the non-dualism of Vedānta and the social reform concerns of his earlier perspective. He devised a grandiose plan to revitalize Hinduism, to expunge it of the aura of pessimism and criticism that it represents a form of escapism from the world, and to share its religious wisdom with the West. Securing a wealthy patron in the person of the Maharajah of Khetri, he planned to attend the World Parliament of Religions in 1893 in Chicago, but before he left he changed his name to Vivekānanda at the suggestion of his generous patron.

While at this international conference, he claimed to represent an ancient order of world renouncers within the tradition of Śaṅkara, and proceeded to give a dynamic address on the universal truth of Hinduism, which made him a celebrity at the conference and in India when his speech was published in the newspapers of his country. A subsequent lecture tour of America enabled him to attract followers, and he eventually established the Vedānta Society in New York in 1895 to be followed by chapters in Boston and London.

Returning to India in 1897 to continue his program of reform and revitalization of Hinduism, he met with initial opposition from the group that he had left behind. Vivekānanda taught that Advaita Vedānta represented the universal form of religion. He also preached a message of tolerance, non-sectarianism, the need for karma yoga (a path of positive action for social welfare), and emphasized that the practice of asceticism must be concerned with the present world and solutions for its many problems. Thus the renouncers of the movement must be servants of all human beings regardless of social status. In his writings he established a clever dichotomy between India and the West. The former was characterized as spiritual, intuitive, religious, tolerant and harmonious, whereas the West represented the mostly negative characteristics of materialism, hedonism, secularism, rationalism and intolerance. Not only did Advaita Vedānta represent the pinnacle of Hinduism and India's national identity, it also encompassed the truth embodied in all religions. Halbfass refers to Vivekānanda's thought as Vedāntic inclusivism, a philosophy that formed the framework and basis for his encounter with the West.[32] By means of the force of his personality and powers of persuasion, Vivekānanda was able to overcome the initial opposition of his former followers, and he founded the Rāmakrishna Mission on May 1, 1897.

With financial assistance from his Western disciples, he purchased land to build a center for the Math and Mission near Calcutta in 1898. By the following year, the Rāmakrishna Math and Mission had become an international organization devoted to active service in the world, and the leadership was transferred from Vivekānanda to his Hindu and Western disciples. The first leader of the Math was Swami Brahmānanda, who was also later appointed to lead the Rāmakrishna Mission just six months before Vivekānanda's death in 1902.

32Wilhelm Halbfass, *India and Europe: An Essay in Understanding* (Albany: State University of New York Press, 1988), pp. 228-229.

Vivekānanda's emphasis on social service was less stressed by his successors, who tended to retrieve the earlier importance of devotional religion. In part, this change of course keep the movement out of the Indian struggle for independence from British rule.

Influenced by the work of Anthony F. C. Wallace, Pangborn argues that the movement established by Vivekānanda can be called a revitalization movement for the following reasons: it seeks to restore vitality to old traditions in order to enhance present spirituality and to encourage social reform; an attempt to stimulate the culture by incorporating alien notions; the efficacious use of a messianic motif to stimulate personal and cultural transformation.[33] Pangborn's position is superior to other types of classification. We can exclude calling The Rāmakrishna Math and Mission either thaumaturgical or utopian because it is not concerned with healings, miracles, magic, and does not believe that society can be remade by human beings into a utopian society.[34] It is also not a revolutionist nor manipulationist movement. With relation to the former type of movement, it eschews the possibility of a radically transformed future and return to some ideal social reality. It is not a manipulationist movement because worship is important and communal life is not unimportant. The Rāmakrishna Math and Mission does share some features with conversionist, introversionist and reformist movements. Like the introversionist movement, it stresses inner purity within the group, and, similar to the conversionist movement, it emphasizes a subjective experience. It is also reformist in spirit and function because it wants to change the world around it. Therefore, the revitalization typology is useful, if one does not press it too rigidly or exclusively.

RELIGIOUS EXPERIMENTS

Brief mention was made previously of the spiritual odyssey of Rāmakrishna. In order to comprehend the phenomena discussed in subsequent chapters, it is wise to review his quest or, more accurately, his experiments with religious truth. These experiments never lead to a true synthesis of diverse religious paths,[35] although it did promote a catholic attitude, at least in a qualified sense.

Unlike the impression given by his biographers, Rāmakrishna's spiritual odyssey did not move in a straight line, rather it proceeded in a more serpentine manner. The early years of Rāmakrishna's religious odyssey were made without a spiritual guide, and were characterized by a frenzied devotional quest for Kālī. A series of *gurus* (teachers) were to follow in subsequent years. Due to the influence of Vivekānanda, the biography of Rāmakrishna written by Saradānanda arranged his religious experiences as a progression to *nirvikalpa samādhi* of

[33]Pangborn, pp. 99-100.

[34]See Bryan Wilson, *Magic and the Millennium: A Sociological Study of Religious Movements of Protest Among Tribal and Third-World Peoples* (London: Heinemann, 1973).

[35]In contrast, Matchett perceives a coherent synthesis in which is embodied an agnosticism because Rāmakrishna's experience of ultimate reality yields no information for normal consciousness, p. 173.

Vedānta as the culmination of his quest.[36] Although Rāmakrishna practiced other disciplines, he remained a devotee of Kālī throughout his adult life, even though he expressed his teachings in Vedāntic terminology. It is no surprise that his Vedānta was tinged with Tantra and *bhakti* (devotion) sentiment. In reading Rāmakrishna's recorded conversation and his negative opinion of intellectual activity, an inference that can be drawn is that his impure Advaita Vedānta was simply a convenient means of explaining his various experiments. This does not imply that he was insincere in his convictions. But deep in his heart, he was always a *bhakta* (devotee) of Kālī, the primary focus of his existence. As we will see, his non-dualism identified Brahman and Kālī as one reality. Therefore, the biographical accounts of his followers are a bit misleading, and we should not take the notion of a progressive quest culminating in Vedāntic realization with credulous acceptance.

The first teacher of Rāmakrishna of any consequence was Bhairavi Brahmani (also referred to as Yogeśvarī), an older woman with disheveled hair, dressed in the ochre colored robes of a world-renouncer. Beginning in 1861, she guided Rāmakrishna through the rigors of Tantra for about three years, and gave him the discipline necessary to make spiritual progress. Another itinerant religious teacher named Jatadhari, a devotee of Rāma as a child (Rāmalala), encountered Rāmakrishna around 1864. This wandering Vaishnava initiated Rāmakrishna into the Vaishnava *sādhana* (practice, discipline), which culminated in Rāmakrishna's vision of the child Rāma. Toward the end of 1864, another world-renouncer visited Rāmakrishna named Totāpurī, a naked ascetic of the Advaita Vedānta school. He enabled Rāmakrishna to reach *nirvikalpa samādhi,* the highest realization in Vedānta in which one's consciousness is free of all conceptual forms, after the Master was able to transcend his image of Kālī by his powers of conscious discrimination. Toward the end of 1866, Rāmakrishna had a vision of a figure he assumed to be Muhammad, after being instructed by Govinda Rai in Islam. An experience of Jesus was gained by Rāmakrishna in November of 1874, while he viewed a picture of the Madonna and Child. He later had a vision of Jesus in the *panchavati*, a grove of sacred trees where he meditated.

Because of his spiritual odyssey, Rāmakrishna developed a catholic viewpoint toward other world religions. Good examples of his attitude are the following quotations:

> I realize that there is only one God toward whom all are travelling; but the paths are different.[37]
>
> God can be realized through all paths. All religions are true.[38]

---

[36]For a similar observation see Walter G. Neevel, Jr., "The Transformation of Śrī Rāmakrishna," in *Hinduism: New Essays in the History of Religions,* ed. Bardwell L. Smith (Leiden: E. J. Brill, 1976; reprint 1982), p. 67.

[37]M, pp. 129, 265, 191.

[38]Ibid., pp. 111, 191.

From these quotations of Rāmakrishna, we can draw two major conclusions: all religions are true and each represents a legitimate path to reality, and there is a harmony of world religions. This does not mean that all religions are identical; rather, they are equivalent. Rāmakrishna's conviction is based on his inner experiences and verifies his doctrine that all religions lead to the same goal. Thus his subjective experiences produced the needed justification of his catholic attitude.[39] A corollary to his conviction that all paths to salvation lead to self-realization and are true was his belief that the absolute and relative are of equal value.[40] This will be explained further in chapter three.

The catholic attitude of Rāmakrishna is explained by Swami Saradānanda as follows: "After attaining perfection according to all the faiths, the Master had the firm conviction that all religions are true–all faiths are but so many paths."[41] Saradānanda comprehended the meaning of Rāmakrishna's incarnation in terms of his catholic attitude. Saradānanda asserted that Rāmakrishna became incarnated to end the decline of all faiths and terminate quarrels among religions.[42] But did Rāmakrishna himself perfectly practice the faiths enumerated?

There is no direct evidence to suggest that Rāmakrishna intended to save other faiths. He never, for instance, appeared to practice Islam or Christianity in any complete manner for any length of time. There is no evidence that his understanding of these monotheistic religions ever developed beyond a superficial comprehension of their symbols and teachings. With his mystical experiences of Muhammad and Jesus, Rāmakrishna seems to have converted them into acceptable Hindus. As Pangborn observes, Rāmakrishna encountered Muhammad and Jesus on his own terms and not on their bases.[43] We have noted already that Rāmakrishna was not a fully educated individual by any formal type of institutional measurement, although he was not an ignorant dolt, and that the cultural changes occurring in Calcutta in the nineteenth century made absolutely no impact upon him. If he was unaware and untouched with what was happening in his own culture, it seems very improbable that he would have any deep awareness of foreign religions. Moreover, there is no evidence to suggest that he ever read the Qur'ān or New Testament or had them read extensively to him. How can we make sense of Rāmakrishna's apparent tolerant attitude? According to Halbfass, Rāmakrishna's tolerant attitude to Christianity and Islam, for instance, is not necessarily a tolerant position, but is instead an impressive example of inclusivism.[44]

---

[39]Peter Schreiner, "Sri Ramakrishna und Ramana Mahrshi als Vertreter moderner indischer Mystik," *Rausch-Ekstase-Mystik: Grenzformen religiöser Erhafrunq*, ed. Hubert Cancik (Düsseldorf: Patmos Verlag, 1978), p. 64.

[40]Jan Gonda, *Die Religionen Indiens: II der jüngere Hinduismus* (Stuttgart: W. Kohlhammer Verlag, 1963), p. 313.

[41]Saradananda, I: 343.

[42]Ibid., I: 343.

[43]Ibid., I: 343.

[44]Halbfass, p. 227.

Even though Rāmakrishna was personally unaffected to any significant degree by the historical changes occurring around him, he was aware and critical of the social and religious program advocated by the Brāhmo Samāj. His criticism was based on his perception of the relationship between Kālī and the world, her plaything and manifestation of her divine nature. Since the world was a divine manifestation of the goddess, it was not in need of social and religious reforms, mere examples of worldly attachment and non-receptive to change. Moreover, the reform program of the Brāhmo Samāj was an abstraction for Rāmakrishna, whereas the true value of Hinduism is derived from its natural totality as an eternal religion *(sanātana dharma)* in which no one aspect of the divine is isolated from the vast variety of its many concrete manifestations.[45] A truth embodied by this eternal religion is that Kālī is identical to ultimate reality. Since her *śakti* (creative energy) is manifested in all things and she is the single reality, it follows that she is one, but her aspects are many. If there are many aspects to the single reality, and if she has come to earth in order to play *(līlā)*, it makes sense to try to experience her in as many of her aspects as possible. Therefore, the various and often diametrically opposed systems of religion experienced by Rāmakrishna, whatever the depth of his comprehension or practice, were his attempt to experience the *līlā* of Kālī in as many ways as possible.[46] If the forms of her *līlā* are many, the more paths of salvation experienced the better.

On the other hand, Rāmakrishna entered into the various disciplines playfully. He never asserted that one way was absolutely true and another false. They were all to be experienced and enjoyed. It is as if he was let loose in a spiritual toy store and told to enjoy himself. One is also impressed by the spontaneous manner that he would enter a religion or spiritual discipline. With total freedom and abandon, he simply jumped right into a discipline to enjoy the *līlā* of Kālī.

SENSES OF THE MYSTERIOUS PLAY

Up to this point, the word play has been used in two senses: a dramatic performance and to sport *(līlā)*. Nonetheless, these two senses of play are interrelated in this work. It was Kālī, using Rāmakrishna as her leading actor, who directed and controlled the drama that was staged upon the earth in the nineteenth century. Her direction of this real life drama originated in her divine *līlā* (play). Kālī played with her leading actor, and he also played in turn with her. Therefore, due to its importance in the life of Rāmakrishna, play *(līlā)* is the theme of this interpretative study of his life and one of the major threads running through his life. We will attempt to demonstrate that *līlā* can serve as a hermeneutical key to unlock the meaning of Rāmakrishna's life.

Because *līlā* (play) is the overall theme of this work, I will define it more fully in the next chapter. Besides *līlā*, another important thread that runs through Rāmakrishna's life is the significance of the feminine. Thus we will look at his relationship to Kālī, women in general, his wife and the relation between play

---

[45]M, p. 1024.

[46]A similar point is made by Neevel, p. 83.

and the feminine element. Then, we will examine two important aspects of Rāmakrishna's behavior: madness and humor. At times in his life, Rāmakrishna was as crazy as the Mad Hatter of Lewis Carroll's classic work. A wonderful sense of humor emerges from the diary of M, which became *The Gospel of Sri Rāmakrishna* compiled from 1882 to 1886. Rāmakrishna's humor elucidates his humanity and how he played with his disciples and others. The mystery in Kālī's *līlā* emerges when we try to view Rāmakrishna as a stranger, which will attempt to capture the sense of awe and wonder of his original circle of disciples, and how they grappled to comprehend the mysterious figure within their midst. A final phenomenon connected with Rāmakrishna's life was his frequent, sudden and wonderous visions.

Throughout this work, we will attempt to keep Rāmakrishna within his cultural context. This will help us comprehend him as a product of his culture. From time to time, it will be necessary to compare some phenomena connected with Rāmakrishna to figures in other religious traditions. The drawing of comparisons with other religious cultures, at least on a modest scale, will aid our comprehension of Rāmakrishna.

Although numerous sources have been used in this work, the simple diary of M will serve as our foremost guide. Thus the four year diary of M and its recording of the Master's words and actions will be considered the most authentic source for this study in subsequent chapters, with a few exceptions. Why should this one work take precedence over other biographical works? It is not because the other works are false. The other biographical accounts of Rāmakrishna's life were composed sometime after his death, and, as already noted, they often bear the imprint of the influence of Vivekānanda. On the other hand, the diary of M was composed soon after his meetings with the Master. The diary was written by an educated and faithful disciple eager to preserve the words of his teacher for future generations, although even it was influenced to an unknown degree by Vivekānanda helping M. As we will see later, M's work recalls his doubts and bewilderment about Rāmakrishna; it records a pious man's struggle to comprehend and not simply report his encounter with an unusual person. Moreover, M does not attempt to make Rāmakrishna an adherent to any single philosophy. Thus M's diary embodies the characteristic of authenticity.

In fact, M's work can be considered a classic of nineteenth-century Hinduism. A religious classic, according to David Tracy,[47] asks questions, initiates individuals into new self-awareness, provokes, challenges, transforms one's horizon of understanding, and may command important decisions. The classic is authoritative, but it does not bind us or threaten us. The classic is authoritative in a non-pejorative sense because it can shatter intrenched personal prejudices, allow for self-discovery, alter the questions that one may ask, and change one's social and existential horizon. The religious classic is a product of the past and the present moment of the interpreter. Between the past and present, there is a movement back and forth between discovery and concealment, an attempt to close the

[47]David Tracy, *The Analogical Imagination: Christian Theology and the Culture of Pluralism* (New York: Crossroads, 1981), pp. 99-229.

gap of distanciation between event and meaning. Since each of these poles–past and present–remain alive, each new encounter with such a text culminates in both a lived experience and a new interpretation. An interpreter, a mediator between past and present, must not be a slave to previous interpretations. A human composition of the past produces disclosure; it speaks to us when we encounter it in the present and determines the questions that the interpreter can ask. Since the religious classic possesses a surplus of meaning, any single interpretation can never capture all its import. Thus an important virtue for any interpreter would have to be humility. It is also wise to acknowledge that all understanding is radically finite and historical. Therefore, hermeneutics is a risky endeavor, yet this is true of any game that one decides to enter. With relation to the drama produced by the *līlā* of Kālī in the nineteenth century some miles north of Calcutta, it is necessary for the interpreter to become a spectator and thus to become a part of the mystery. By one's involvement, enjoyment and absorption in the text depicting the mystery, one becomes refreshed–an apparently worthwhile goal for any game.

Chapter I I

PLAY

From one perspective, an overview of Hindu devotional religion gives one the impression that the deities are actors and actresses playing their parts on the stage of the cosmos, without hoping for raving reviews from their potential critics nor seeking the plaudits of an admiring audience. But are not all thespians motivated by ego gratification, fame, wealth, adulation of adoring fans and personal identity? Human thespians may be motivated by one, all, or a combination of these goals, but various Hindu deities are unmotivated because their actions are pure play, an unmotivated, spontaneous, intentionless, aimless display. Their play is simply awesome and wonderful. Theatrical critics need not attend a divine performance with the intention of writing a critical review for the morning edition of their newspapers. Although one can find a leading actor or actress performing, the play performed by the Hindu deities possesses no purpose, no beginning and no end . When a critic attends such a display no notes need be taken. It is merely necessary to sit back and enjoy the show.

Hindu deities have been putting on a show for centuries. Within the context of devotional Hinduism, one finds several award winning performers. Vishnu, for instance, plays tricks on Manu, the protector of all creatures, by growing from a small fish able to live in a bowl to a continually larger fish needing an ocean to survive in a Matsya *avatāra* episode. Vishnu, as Matsya, warns Manu about the coming cosmic flood, and he appears during the flood as a horned fish to which Manu's ship is tied and the representative creatures of each species are saved.[1] As Vāmana (the Dwarf), Vishnu tricks the demonic Bali, who gained dominion over the cosmos by practicing *tapas* (ascetic austerities), into giving him as much land as he can encompass with three steps. Similar to the three steps of Vishnu in the Rig Veda (1.154.1-6), the god's first step covers the earth, then the heavens, and the third step rests on Bali's head due to a lack of space and pushes the demon into the underworld[2]. In another *avatāra* episode, the uncontrollable demon Hiraṇyakaśipu is granted a boon by the god Brahmā; as a result he cannot be killed during the day or at night, by a god, man or beast, and neither inside nor outside of his palace. Vishnu playfully appears as Narasiṃha, the Man-Lion, at twilight within a pillar of the demon's palace and rips the demonic being to shreds.[3]

---

[1]*Matsya Purāṇa*, Ānandāśrama Sanskrit Series 54 (Poona, 1907), 1.11-34;2.1-19.

[2]*Vāyu Purāṇa* (Bombay: Śrī-Venkaṭeśvara Steam Press, 1895), 2.36.74-86.

[3]*The Śiva Purāṇa*, 4 Vols., Trans. by A Board of Scholars (Delhi: Motilal Banarsidass, 1969-70), Rudra Śāmhitā, 2.5.4-43.

The most playful *avatāra* is Krishna, the divine child and lover.[4] He plays tricks by stealing butter, symbolic of ample love, and sweets from women. With a disdain for social convention and rules, Krishna behaves spontaneously and impetuously by also setting the local cows free, making small children cry, defecating in people's homes and laughing at those who reprimand him. When the demoness Pūtanā offers the infant Krishna her poisoned breasts, the infant sucks the life out of her.[5] Krishna amuses himself by defeating other demonic beings in a spirit of play. As the divine lover and embodiment of beauty, Krishna sexually frolicks with the *gopīs* (cow maidens) in idyllic Vṛndāvana, a divine earthly playground, by performing the *rāsa-līlā* (circle dance), stationing himself between every two *gopīs* by means of his power of *māyā* (illusory, magical power).[6] It is implied in the *Bhāgavata Purāṇa* that Krishna prefers an unnamed *gopī*, who becomes identified as Rādhā in the *Gītagovinda* (twelfth-century C.E.) of Jayadeva. Their love is depicted by Jayadeva as intense, passionate, violent, erotic, comic and a form of divine play *(līlā)*.[7]

Although he is not comparatively as playful as Krishna, Śiva, the ascetic and householder, dances in the spirit of play before the wives of the Pine Forest sages. The wives of the sages become bewitched by the ash covered, naked, erotically dancing deity and in some versions of the myth give themselves sexually to the god.[8] Or Śiva playfully castrates himself and throws his *liṅga* (phallus) upon the earth's surface, which descends into the earth and rises to the sky in order to teach Brahmā and Vishnu, who are both unable to find the end of the *liṅga*, a lesson about the androgynous god's greatness.[9] During the interval between the destruction and reabsorption of one world age and the beginning of a new aeon, the two divine witnesses are present to see the theophany of Śiva's *liṅga*.[10] In another Purāṇic episode, Śiva destroys the horse-sacrifice of Dakṣa, to which he is not invited, with a drop of his sweat, which becomes a prodigious

---

[4]The following works deal with the concept of play in the life of Krishna: John Stratton Hawley, *At Play with Krishna: Pilgrimage Dramas from Brindavan* (Princeton: Princeton University Press, 1981); John Stratton Hawley, *Krishna, The Butter Thief* (Princeton: Princeton University Press, 1983); David R. Kinsley, *The Sword and the Flute: Kālī and Kṛṣṇa, Dark Visions of the Terrible and the Sublime in Hindu Mythology* (Berkeley: University of California Press, 1975); David R. Kinsley, "Without Kṛṣṇa There is No Song," *History of Religions*, 12/2 (November 1972), 149-180; Charles S. J. White, "Krsna as Divine Child," *History of Religions*, 10/2 (1970), 156-177.

[5]*Viṣṇu Purāṇa* (Gorakhpur: Gita Press, n.d.), 5.5.1-23.

[6] Ibid ., 5.13.14-62.

[7] For a discussion of Jayadeva's poem see Carl Olson, "Śrī Lakshmī and Rādhā: The Obsequious Wife and the Lustful Lover," in *The Book of the Goddess Past Present*, ed. Carl Olson (New York: Crossroad Publishing Company, 1983), 124-144.

[8]*The Liṅga Purāṇa* 2 Vols., Trans., by A Board of Scholars (Delhi: Motilal Barnarsidass, 1973), 1.29.1-25.

[9]Ibid., 1.17.32-59.

[10]Stella Kramrisch, *The Dance of Śiva* (Princeton: Princeton University Press, 1981), p. 159.

fire.[11] "Though Dakṣa's sacrifice was part of Śiva's divine play," observes Kramrisch, "it was the culmination of Rudra's aeviternal struggle for recognition by those gods who had been critical of him from the beginning."[12] The effortless and playful way in which Śiva destroys the triple city of the demons with a single arrow that burns the demonic cities is also indicative of his playful, destructive power.[13] Besides the destructive, adulterous and ascetic aspects of Śiva's nature, he is also the playful Naṭarāja, lord of dance.[14] As he dances, Śiva holds a drum in his upper right hand that furnishes the rhythm for his dance and represents the tempo of the universe, the regularity of the seasons, the course of the planets, the repetition of the ages and creates the first forms of existence. The right hand is complemented by the flame of destruction in his upper left hand. Śiva displays the fear-not gesture *(abhava-mudrā)* in his lower right hand, which is complemented by the lower left hand pointing to his upraised foot, representing refuge and salvation.

Vishnu, Krishna, Śiva and other deities received worship from Rāmakrishna. There is, however, no divine figure that compares to the devotion rendered to Kālī by Rāmakrishna. Kālī, naked, immodest, sexually aggressive and terrible in appearance, playfully destroys demons by grinding them with her teeth after emerging from the forehead of the goddess Ambikā in the *Devī-Mahātmya* section of the *Mārkaṇḍeya Purāṇa*,[15] which also depicts her assisting Caṇḍikā destroy the demonic Raktabīja by stretching out her mouth to drink his blood before it fell to the earth and created a duplicate demon. In the *Bhāgavata Purāṇa*, Kālī and her attendants play catch with the severed heads of a band of thieves, whose chieftain tried to kill and offer a saintly man as a sacrificial offering to the Goddess. Throwing the heads of her victims back and forth with her attendants, Kālī is depicted singing, dancing and inebriated from the blood of the thieves.[16] Although this is a rather gruesome scene, it does demonstrate Kālī's wild, mad, awesome, tumultuous and playful nature, features that will be more fully discussed in the next chapter.

Even though the natures of Vishnu, Krishna, Śiva and Kālī differ to some extent, they share the common activity of *līlā* (divine play, sport, dalliance), a pure, intentionless, voluntary activity. Play is an easy, free, spontaneously, unpredictable and purposeless activity, whereas work possesses an intentional character because it strives to laboriously secure some goal related to the worker's

---

[11]*The Śiva Purāṇa*, Rudra Saṁhitā, 2.37.1-68.

[12]Kramrisch, pp. 325-26.

[13]*Matsya Purana*, 129.1-20; 129.36; 128.3-28; *The Śiva Purāṇa*, Rudra Saṁhitā, 5.10.1-28.

[14]Ananda K. Coomaraswamy, *The Dance of Siva* (New York: Farrar, Straus & Giroux, 1953; reprint, New Delhi: Sagar Publications, 1971), pp. 66-79.

[15]*The Mārkaṇḍeya Purāṇa*, trans. F. E. Pargiter (Calcutta: The Asiatic Society, 1904; reprint, Delhi: Indological Book House, 1969), 84.1-25; 89.29-37.

[16]*The Bhāgavata Purāṇa*, 5 Vols., Trans. Ganesh Vasudeo Tagare (Delhi: Motilal Banarsidass, 1976), 5.9.12-20.

needs and well-being.[17] Since play creates no products nor wealth, it is an unproductive activity or, even more, a pure waste of time, energy and skill.[18] The need to work in order to achieve a goal is considered a shortcoming. Because they are complete, needing and desiring nothing, and free from the laws of cause and effect, Hindu deities do not need to work; their actions are simply play.[19] The essence of divine play is captured by Kinsley:

> To play is to be unfettered and unconditioned, to perform actions that are intrinsically satisfying to sing, dance, and laugh. To play is to step out of the ordinary world of the humdrum, to enter a special, magical world where one can revel in the superfluous.[20]

Besides expressing the transcendent completeness and freedom of the Hindu deities, play also suggests an aloofness of the divine beings towards the world. "They create the world in play and involve themselves only incidentally or accidentally with the ongoing world order."[21] Devoid of any selfish motives, purpose or compulsion to create the world, the concept of *līlā* implies that Hindu deities are not responsible for what they create, nor do they have to be concerned with the moral consequences of their playful actions. A distinction can be made between the inner and outer forms of divine *līlā*. The latter type of play enables human beings easy access to comprehend it, whereas the former type of play relates to the mystery of the cosmic process and origin of the universe.[22] Thus the universe is a mere toy or plaything of the deities. And it often becomes their playground where they can spontaneously display their creativity and playfulness.

Whether the divine beings are destroying, maintaining or creating, their activity is not serious. Only human creativeness or destructiveness are determined by a seriousness of purpose . For divine beings, play is a mere recreation, an activity without purpose. To be serious is to be transported in the opposite direction of play, a destination that leads to bondage rather than freedom .

When the deities play they are absorbed in what they are doing. Lost within the splendor of themselves and their spontaneous activity, the deities do not consciously intend to play or to behave in a playful manner because play possesses its own essence, which is independent of the conscious intention of those play-

---

17Ananda K. Coomaraswamy, "Līlā," *Journal of the American Oriental Society*, 61 (1941), p. 98.

18Roger Caillois, *Man, Play and Games*, Trans. Meyer Barash (New York: The Free Press, 1961), pp. 5-6.

19Kinsley, *The Sword and the Flute*, p. 73.

20Ibid., p. 74.

21Ibid., p. 73.

22Walther Eidlitz, *Kṛṣṇa-Caitanya Sein Leben und Seine Lehre*, Stockholm Studies in Comparative Religion 7 (Stockholm: Almqvist & Wiksell, 1968), p. 69.

ing.[23] Not to think about it, but to just do it. This is what makes play what it is.

KĀLĪ AND PLAY

Those who have directed a theatrical production or acted in a play know what a tremendous amount of work such a venture demands of one's time, energy and talent. The play produced and directed by Kālī–the life and antics of Rāmakrishna–does not strangely involve work, which, as noted, is a limiting and purposeful activity. The production starring Rāmakrishna directed by Kālī is executed out of pure, spontaneous, unpredictable play.

Kālī is forever playing, whether creating, preserving or destroying. She is identical to Brahman and vice versa, representing one and the same playful reality.[24] Just as the Goddess can appear in different forms, she also plays in a variety of ways. Sometimes she descends to earth to appear, for example, in human form. Not only is the Goddess real for Rāmakrishna, but her play *(līlā)* is also real.[25] This suggests that Rāmakrishna does not completely accept the illusory quality of divine play. To accept only the reality of Kālī (Brahman) and conclude that the world is simply a dream is, according to Rāmakrishna, a very difficult path to follow.[26] This would necessarily mean that divine play is also unreal. Rāmakrishna is suggesting that this is a dangerous and difficult path that only a very few can follow. He seems to be suggesting that it is easier to accept the reality of divine play.

During his life, Kālī played a game of hide-and-seek with Rāmakrishna, which caused him both joy and suffering. Kālī is like the granny, the leader in the Indian version of hide-and-seek, who hides herself after bandaging the eyes of the players. When a player finds and touches her, the individual's bandage is removed, his eyes uncovered, and he is released from the game.[27] However, Kālī continues to play and keeps one bound to the world so that one can continue to enjoy the game. Thus the Goddess controls the game. She is yet, on the other hand, under the control of her devotee because she is tied, according to Rāmakrishna, by the love of her players.[28] Therefore, the game that one enters with Kālī is a kind of team sport in which the players need one another and mutually enjoy their common sporting.

Kālī plays by means of her *māyā* (supernatural skill, magical or illusory power). Due to this creative power, Rāmakrishna thinks that in the final analysis he is subject to her control.[29] Her cosmic, beguiling, magical power pulls one

---

[23]Hans-Georg Gadamer, *Truth and Method*, Trans. Garrett Barden & John Cumming (New York: Crossroad Publishing Company, 1982), p. 92.

[24]M, p. 134.

[25]Ibid., p. 238.

[26]Ibid., p. 355.

[27]Ibid., note 6, p. 136.

[28]Ibid,., p. 355.

[29]Ibid., p. 211.

inextricably into her game. Rāmakrishna comprehends himself metaphorically as a puppet on a string and Kālī as the master puppeteer. The individual puppet is thus without recourse except to take refuge in the divine sport and enjoy the fun. What makes the game especially enjoyable is its loving nature. Like an intoxicated swimmer, the human lover sometimes swims, descends, or rises to the surface in the ocean of divine consciousness.[30] The lover of Kālī possesses complex emotions and expresses these feelings in a variety of ways: laughter, weeping, and the joy of dancing and singing.

The most wonderful form of Kālī's play, for Rāmakrishna, is when she decides to play as a human being.[31] This is the most lucid form of her love, which is why she descends to earth to play. She does this strictly for the sake of her devotees, which is necessary not for the Goddess, but solely for the benefit of her devotees. Since human beings can only love her in her human form, Kālī incarnates herself in order for humans to shower her with affection and play her game.[32] This is no defect on the Goddess' part; it is rather a manifestation of her loving and playful nature. Thus it is on earth that Kālī plays, fascinates and dazzles her devotees through the person of Rāmakrishna.

PLAY OF A CHILD

According to his biographers, Rāmakrishna enjoyed playing the parts of divine beings in theatrical performances since early childhood. In a sense, he never did stop playing the role of a god throughout his life. Another predominant characteristic of Rāmakrishna was his child-like behavior even as an adult. Considering his childish behavior as an adult, an unsympathetic observer might conclude that Rāmakrishna never did grow up or mature to the point of becoming a responsible mature person. Even though he held a position as a temple priest and got married, Rāmakrishna never did become a sober and responsible member of Hindu society. He rather created his own society–a religious fellowship with himself as the hub. This spiritual fellowship was created through his play. If one returns to the biographical accounts of his early life, one will perceive a consistent manifestation of the spirit of play in Rāmakrishna's life even to the point where throat cancer threatened to take his life. Thus the spirit of play was not entered into by Rāmakrishna on a part-time basis, but it was rather ingrained into his very existence; he continuously lived the spirit of play throughout his life.

Rāmakrishna's biographers reported that he played the role of Śiva in a local play in a very convincing manner to such an extent that he became lost in his part. While absorbed in his role, Rāmakrishna went into a trance, and had a vision of the ascetic god. He also played other roles of divine beings, especially the youthful sports of Krishna. Rather then attend classes with his friends, Rāmakrishna cut school to play with his boyhood friends, like the youthful cowherder Krishna, forming with his companions a dramatic company that per-

---

[30]Ibid., p. 277.
[31]Ibid., p. 826.
[32]Ibid., p. 382.

formed plays based on themes from the *Rāmāyaṇa* and *Mahābhārata* epics.[33] During his performance, Rāmakrishna often became overwhelmed with emotion and fell into trances. These dramatic roles suggest a kind of preparation for his later adult performance as an incarnation.

Rāmakrishna was not only a magnet for the young boys of the village, but he also held an attraction, according to his biographers, for the local women, in whose company he tended to spend more time after his brother left for Calcutta to assume his priestly duties. Women came to Rāmakrishna's home to hear him recite a holy text, sing, mimic the behavior of others and imitate especially the voices of women. This playful attitude seemed to remind older women of the child Krishna, whereas younger women perceived him to possess characteristics of adolescent Krishna.[34] Sometimes he donned the clothing and assumed the mannerisms of a woman. He would, for instance, disguise himself as a local girl carrying a waterjug, and go about undetected by those who had known him all his life. The young Rāmakrishna was so adept at his art that he challenged a neighbor named Durgadas, a strict adherent of the *purdah* system of secluding women in a part of a home, that he could easily gain access to the women's quarters. After disguising himself as a woman and passing the questions asked by Durgadas, Rāmakrishna was allowed to enter the company of the secluded women. When his brother called for him, Rāmakrishna answered from the women's quarters giving his location to the amazement of his defeated opponent.[35] Since sex roles are clearly defined in India and often symbolized by one's clothing, to abrogate one's sexual identity was often a matter of amusing playfulness.[36] As we will notice later in subsequent chapters, Rāmakrishna's feminine role playing continued into his adult years.

Rāmakrishna's child-like behavior continued into his adult life. It is reported by M that the Master was happy in the company of children, singing to them frivolous songs to entertain them.[37] Rāmakrishna's behavior suggests in part that he was still very much like them in spirit. Rāmakrishna offered a more theological answer to his childish behavior: one becomes like a child after realizing the Goddess, who plays with the universe by creating, preserving and destroying it much like a child does with its toy house. Since the Goddess has a childish nature, one acquired a similar nature by meditating upon her.[38] Within Rāmakrishna's religious world-view, it was permissible for an adult to act like a child. Rāmakrishna, for instance, wanted to attend the Wilson Circus on November 15, 1882. On the way to the circus, Rāmakrishna manifested the excitement and joy of a child anticipating a wonderful event.[39] Rāmakrishna's child-like demeanor suggests the innocence of his play. To become true devotees

---

[33]*Life of Sri Ramakrishna*, p. 23.
[34]Ibid., p. 26.
[35]Ibid., p. 28.
[36]Hawley, *At Play with Krishna* p. 111.
[37]M, p. 490.
[38]Ibid., p. 176.
[39]Ibid., p. 154.

of the Goddess and Rāmakrishna's ardent disciples means that one must be a child, free to play at any time whenever the call is given to enter the game.

The Master's child-like spirit continued even after he learned of his cancer. Turned within himself with devotees seated near him, Rāmakrishna sat in a completely silent room with his face beaming, as if he were not in excruciating pain. Flowers and garlands were lovingly placed before him by devotees. He picked up a flower and touched it to several parts of his body. M interpreted the minds of his devotees: "To the devotees he seemed a child playing with flowers."[40] Thus not even his cancer could interrupt his playfulness. In fact, his cancer was a form of Kālī's *līlā*, a way of sporting through his body.[41] Thus his cancer was not to be lamented, but rather it needed to be accepted as part of the divine sport *(līlā)*.

Rāmakrishna was not the only saint or incarnation to manifest a playful nature. Another good example from the Bengali area was Caitanya of the sixteenth century to be discussed in subsequent chapters. An even earlier example was manifested in the late thirteenth century in Mahārāṣṭra by Guṇḍam Rāuḷ (also called Gosāvī), believed to be an *avatāra* by the Mahānubhāva sect. The Gosāvī enjoyed playing games with children, like hide-and-seek and touch-the-post.[42] He played with the images of deities in the local temples and his own reflection in water.[43] Gosāvī played with the local animals. He would, for instance, frighten cows to such an extent that they would run away.[44] He pretended to be afraid of a dog in his path; he pretended to milk a stone or imagined that a rock was a horse.[45] The local people appeared to indulge his playfulness. Local proprietors let him play, for example, with their coins and gold, and at a water stand he placed his two feet into two water jars.[46] Gosāvī was also a teaser when he told a local woman named Sādhem that her nose would fall off her face.[47] At another time, he chased the obese Sādhem and caught her when she got her corpulent body stuck in a gate trying to escape from Gosāvī's attack. While stuck in her precarious predicament, Gosāvī grasped her breasts and began to make outrageous comments.[48] In a mock wedding ceremony, Gosāvī played the role of a bridegroom adorned with a nuptial crown and wedding bracelet, and anointed with turmeric.[49] Gosāvī's actions could even be more outrageous: he pretended to be cold and warmed himself over a pile of ashes or held his hands over a lamp,[50] or

---

[40]Ibid., p. 969.

[41]Ibid., pp. 895, 970.

[42]Anne Feldhaus, trans. *The Deeds of God in Ṛddhipur* (New York: Oxford University Press, 1984), 21, also 9, 10, 13.

[43]Ibid., 298, 65, 76, 158, 260, 288.

[44]Ibid., 60, 309.

[45]Ibid., 59, 316, 154.

[46]Ibid., 305, 306, 20.

[47]Ibid., 111.

[48]Ibid., 180.

[49]Ibid., 224.

[50]Ibid., p. 261.

he reproached his buttocks after he farted,[51] or he sat on his thinking rock deciding where to go next.

THE DANCER

By dancing, one expresses oneself, celebrates life and imitates the deities. As already noted, Krishna, Śiva and Kālī are expert dancers. Their dancing is directly related to their awesome creative and destructive powers and is a lucid manifestation of their play *(līlā)*. When Rāmakrishna danced he also embodied the spirit of play.

On June 18, 1833, the Master was invited to a religious festival by Mani Sen, the custodian of the temple of Rādhā-Krishna at Pānihāti not far from Calcutta, called The Festival of the Flattened Rice, which had been historically inaugurated by Raghunāth Dās, a disciple of the sixteenth-century Bengali saint Caitanya. When his carriage arrived at the site of the festival, Rāmakrishna raced into the crowd to the utter amazement of his devotees, joining those performing *kīrtana*. The Master danced oblivious of the world. Since he occasionally stood still, transfixed in *samādhi*, a devotee supported him so that he would not fall to the ground and get hurt. The dancing and fervor of Rāmakrishna seemed to infect the crowd as they swayed, danced and chanted Krishna's name until the air reverberated with the divine name.[52] At other times, Rāmakrishna's dancing was somewhat less public and took place in his room with devotees or members of the Brāhmo Samāj. Often others danced and sang around the Master, who represented the very hub of the dance. This form of dance was reminiscent of Krishna's famous circle dance *(rāsa līlā)* with the *gopīs*. When recording these dance episodes M continually refers to the "ecstasy of divine love" and "intoxication with the love of God" to describe the mood of the participants.[53] As the dancers circled around the Master, both parties would forget the world.[54] When Rāmakrishna played the role of ecstatic dancer some important things were occurring.

By means of his dancing, Rāmakrishna was pulling others from their worldly attachments, representing the spirit of renunciation embodied within the *kīrtana*. The participants were wrenched from their fixed social location and transported into a realm of pure bliss and love, a kind of foretaste of heavenly existence. By dancing around the spiritual magnetic force of Rāmakrishna, the participants were integrated into a spontaneous community of pure love, even though its duration might only last as long as the dance itself. Therefore, the dance *līlā* of Rāmakrishna possessed relational and loving characteristics. The pure love characteristic of the *kīrtana* was an egoless, selfless, all-embracing kind of love. Dance was appropriate in a theatrical play, according to the

---

[51]Ibid., p. 101.
[52]M., p. 253.
[53]Ibid., pp. 599, 153.
[54]Ibid., p. 312.

Nāṭyaśāstra,[55] when a lover was near or when a scene was connected with love. In this way, the dance became a source of joy. Thus the *līlā* of Rāmakrishna met classical dramatic criteria, although it probably did so unintentionally.

Besides love, the dancing of Rāmakrishna elicited an emotional mood *(rasa)* and allowed it to overflow in himself and others, a flow that enabled one to attain satisfaction and pleasure, according to classical theory.[56] It also had the effect of allowing one to forget oneself, to lose oneself in the overflowing emotion, joy and love. Moreover, the dancing of Rāmakrishna encouraged others to participate in the mood *(rasa)* created by the *kīrtana* performances.

The dancing of Rāmakrishna and the mood that it created was contagious. M gave an excellent illustration of the contagious influence of the incarnational dancer: When the musician began to play and sing Rāmakrishna arose to dance, while improvising and reciting poems about the ecstatic love of the divine, with arms extended. After falling into a trance condition, he sat down, later arose again to dance, and periodically went into deep trance states while dancing. The musician and devotees were carried away by their emotions. Within the deepest states of trance, Rāmakrishna could not utter a word and his body became transfixed, forming a center around which his devotees danced encircling their master.[57] Rāmakrishna was not merely the center of attraction, but he was also the magnet around which the others revolved. In this example, his dancing, singing and the subsequent mood created were not only felt by his devotees, but by the larger crowd. The contagiousness of *līlā* and the overflowing of *rasa* engulfed all within its path. Everyone within the radius of its infectious influence was engulfed by the *līlā* of pure pleasure and love. It was as if a dam was broken by the *līlā* of Rāmakrishna and selfless love was allowed to flow and drench everyone in its path.

By means of his dancing, Rāmakrishna literally touched others and transformed them. While dancing and singing, Rāmakrishna frequently passed into *samādhi,* suddenly standing still, his eyes fixed, his face beaming, and his body supported by a disciple. The ecstatic trances of the Master sometimes caused others to have a similar experience, or they might weep like little children calling for their Divine Mother.[58] Besides his dancing, Rāmakrishna achieved a similar result with his physical touch. Narendranāth, for example, related his experience after the Master touched him with his foot: "'I saw with my eyes open that all the things of the room together with the walls were rapidly whirling and receding into an unknown region and my I-ness together with the whole universe was, as it were, going to vanish in an all-devouring great void.'"[59] This was further evidence of the power of *līlā* and its ability to transport one into a transcendental realm. Rāmakrishna's *līlā* drew others out of their mundane world into a

---

[55]The Nāṭyaśāstra, 4.313-14.

[56]Ibid., 6.31.

[57]M, p. 509.

[58]Ibid., pp 93, 632, 661.

[59]Saradananda, II: 842; for an account of a devotee being transported into a trance state by the touch of Rāmakrishna, see II: 933.

realm that was so wonderful that it seemed to be a magical world of make-believe, a world that did not exist on land or sea.

By eliciting from the religious imagination of the devotee a make-believe world (which was the only real world from Rāmakrishna's perspective), Rāmakrishna represented the master dancer and magician. The master illusionist or, from another perspective, reality creator did this for nothing but his own delight and the joy of others. The make-believe world was a realm to which one could escape in order to transcend the suffering of the mundane world. Hartt insightfully writes, "The make-believe world is able to internalize man; it can ingest him and thereby take him out of himself."[60] If one heeded its summons, *līlā* allowed one to leave the mundane world and one's egoism behind in order to be fully engaged in divine play.

If Rāmakrishna was a puppet dangling madly on the end of strings controlled by the mad Kālī, he appeared to be under the control of a higher power. Yet he gave another impression which complemented the initial vision. He also danced before the Goddess as a free spirit. He leaped with unbounded joy and love before her image or vision.

PLAY, BONDAGE AND LIBERATION

Since the Goddess created the world in the spirit of play, she has also created good and evil, happiness and sorrow, and virtue and vice. To someone who objected that there seemed to be more evil, suffering, vice and ignorance in the world than their opposites, Rāmakrishna replied in essence that the world is like a game in which opposites like joy and sorrow, knowledge and ignorance, and good and evil are necessary because without the negative opposites of the positive things of life no game is possible. If there was no sin and suffering within the world, the game of the Goddess could not continue.[61] If one thus asked Rāmakrishna why Kālī created, for instance, evil and ignorance, his answer was simply that it represented her mysterious play *(līlā)*. Replying to the question of why the Goddess created ignorance, Rāmakrishna replied that we cannot possibly appreciate light without darkness, we cannot grasp happiness without suffering, and knowledge of the good is only possible because we know about evil.[62] Thus opposites created in play by means of *māyā* (magical power) were not mutually contradictory, but they were rather complementary.

If the play *(līlā)* of the Goddess was responsible for evil and ignorance, it was also the origin of one's bondage and entanglement in the world.[63] Since the Goddess bound one with the shackles of illusion *(māyā)*, one must take refuge with her. This was not, however, to be lamented. In fact, one's groping within

---

[60]Julian N. Hartt, *The Restless Quest* (Philadelphia: United Church Press, 1975), p. 128.

[61]M, pp. 436, 211.

[62]Ibid., p. 216 and also on evil a similar reply on p. 97.

[63]Ibid., p. 614.

the grand illusion *(mahāmāyā)* was really great fun.[64] Because it was difficult to find one's way through the grand illusion created by the Goddess, it seemed plausible to renounce the world, a path that Rāmakrishna appeared to advocate at times. Yet he also apparently contradicted himself when he said that one should follow the trail of *līlā* in order to reach the absolute *(nitya)*. What he suggested was that we initially realized the Goddess and then descended to the relative plane to live in the company of others with a love-filled mind concentrated on Kālī.[65] Like the complementary worldly products of the Goddess' *māyā* (creative power), the path of liberation involved an ascent of the mundane and then a descent into the world in order to frolic in the game of life.

Rāmakrishna is discovered following his own advice, for instance, in the confines of his own room, which he unintentionally transformed into a miniature amusement park for all visitors to enjoy. The Master was found enjoying laughter with young boys in his room, "as if it were a mart of joy."[66] M described the same joyful and playful atmosphere with the Master at the center of it, even though Rāmakrishna's injured arm was still bandaged from a fall. His room vibrated with bliss, according to M, because of the incessant spiritual talk, singing, dancing and flights by Rāmakrishna into *samādhi*.[67] If the world was a place of mirth framed in illusion, Rāmakrishna's room was a microcosm of the illusory, mirthful, fun world. The devotees who flocked to his room daily gave the appearance of eagerly attending a never ending festival.

Separated within the self-contained space of Rāmakrishna's room, the .Master and his devotees isolated themselves from the distractive events and evil of the outside world. Due to the presence of the playful *avatāra* (incarnation), the room was consecrated by its contact with the sacred person, becoming a sacred zone of play. That the site of so many *kīrtanas* was a sacred place in the minds of his devotees was proven by the fact that after Rāmakrishna's death his room became a shrine where subsequent generations of devotees could visit to share in the circumambient holiness of the place.

The blissful atmosphere created in Rāmakrishna's room shared some essential features of a religious festival.[68] The singing, dancing and ecstatic trance states suggest the excesses of an ordinary festival. Although there was no destruction and waste common to many regular festivals, one does find revelry and joy in Rāmakrishna's room. The devotees of Rāmakrishna were probably attracted to him because of his charisma and the aura of his religious persona. Their daily visits to their spiritual master also provided them, however, with a break from their conventional social lives or a brief vacation, an opportunity to

---

[64]Ibid., p. 116.

[65]Ibid., p. 257.

[66]Ibid., p. 90.

[67]Ibid., p. 406.

[68]See Harvey Cox, *The Feast of Fools: A Theological Essay on Festivity & Fantasy* (Cambridge: Harvard University Press, 1969), p. 23. For a recent informative selection of essays on Indian festival see the following: Guy R. Welbon and Glenn E. Yocum eds. *Religious Festivals in South India and Sri Lanka* (New Delhi: Manohar Publications, 1982).

break loose and express themselves. By playing in this microcosm of mirth, the devotees and Rāmakrishna were affirming life. Despite evil, suffering, ignorance and death, the gaiety characteristic of Rāmakrishna's room was a manifestation of an affirmation of human existence lived within the *māyā* of Kālī. Although one does not find that things were done in reverse like a normal festival, what transpired within the confines of Rāmakrishna's room represented a sharp contrast to the humdrum everyday life of the devotees. Emotions were allowed to overflow to excessive levels creating a profound change within the individual. As described by M, the scenes in Rāmakrishna's room were somewhat chaotic, which suggests a return to primordial chaos in the sense that it was rediscovered and newly created. The festive atmosphere created by Rāmakrishna within his room provided an opportunity to also rediscover and reestablish one's relationship to the Goddess and to express the joy of this poignant event.

The festive atmosphere of Rāmakrishna's residence was often enhanced by music to accompany the singing and dancing. Not only did music bring pleasure to the ears, but it possessed the potential to break the cycle of earthly existence, bring one into contact with ultimate reality and aid in the painless and pleasurablc attainment of liberation.[69] Within the confines of Rāmakrishna's abode, music invoked the presence of the divine, created an inner calm, united the participants in a joyful experience and allowed their inner emotions to overflow.

Saradānanda, a biographer of the Bengali Master, summarized the topic of this chapter when he referred to Rāmakrishna as the very embodiment of *līlā* (play), even though he acknowledged that Rāmakrishna was a madman and "hopelessly good-for-nothing."[70] Play itself was useless, intentionless and sheer enjoyment. Although Rāmakrishna possessed no social utility in the sense of a contributor to social well-being and development, others were attracted to this strange man, who could charm, amaze, and mystify one with his voice, antics and simple presence.

---

[69]See Donna Marie Wulff, "On Practicing Religiously: Music as Sacred in India," in *Sacred Sound: Music in Religious Thought and Practice*, ed. Joyce Irwin, Thematic Studies 50/1 (Chico, CA: Scholars Press, 1984), pp. 149-72.

[70]Saradananda, I:213. The most extensive study of the concept of play in Western culture is provided by Johan Huizinga in his classic work entitled *Homo Ludens: A Study of the Play-Element in Culture* (Boston: Beacon Press, 1955). According to Huizinga, there is a sense and meaning to the activity of play, even though it is an irrational, non-serious and superfluous activity that human beings share in common with animals. This voluntary activity is characterized by freedom, the utter absorption of the player and the fun—its essence—of participating. Huizinga defines the main characteristics of play as not representing real life, being an interlude in our ordinary lives, being distinct with relation to its locality and duration because play is limited to time and place, embodying an element of tension that suggests its uncertainty, and possessing rules and secrecy. Huizinga's conception of play lacks the purposeless, spontaneous and limitless nature of the Hindu concept of *līlā*.

Chapter III

THE FEMININE THREAD

In the previous chapter the connection between play and Kālī was discussed. Since she assumed such a crucial role in the life of Rāmakrishna, it is essential that we investigate more fully the Master's understanding of her nature and his relationship to her. It will be discovered that Rāmakrishna's relationship to Kālī influenced his relationship to mortal women in general and his wife in particular, topics that must also be examined if one is to gain a more complete understanding of the relationship between the Master and the feminine element. The evidence suggests that Rāmakrishna had important relationships with women of different social status throughout his life. In fact, we are informed that women were attracted to him. Since Rāmakrishna could not be ranked among the most handsome men of Calcutta society because of his frail, thin physical appearance, gaps between his teeth, unphotogenic face and odd behavior, and since he was already married during the period of his greatest impact, the reason for his attraction to women was certainly not his physical beauty nor marital availability. The attraction of women to Rāmakrishna was more spiritual and mysterious. We know that he had visions of Hindu goddesses (and the importance of visions will be more fully explored in chapter seven). And he even assumed the social roles, appearance, behavior and speech of women during his life, which renders it necessary to examine the relationship between play *(līlā)* and the feminine in his life. Thus this chapter assumes for the items enumerated that one cannot understand the teachings and behavior of Rāmakrishna unless one grasps the significance of the feminine in his life. It is as if a feminine thread runs throughout his life giving it a unity and meaning.

THE DIVINE MOTHER

The image of Kālī in the temple of Dakshineswar north of Calcutta depicts her with a garland of human heads hanging from her neck, severed human hands dangling from her waistband, blood flowing from her mouth; her color is black and she holds a sword.[1] What sense can an objective and empathic investigator make of these terrifying and awesome features of the Goddess? And what sense did Rāmakrishna make of them?

Kālī's image and mythology inform us that she is closely associated with blood, the sap of life. Not only does she constantly drink blood, but she also receives blood offerings from her devotees in order to satisfy her insatiable thirst

---

[1]M, p. 135.

for the sap of life. She subsists on the blood of her victims and those animals offered to her that satisfy her for a time, although she receives a much greater satisfaction from the sacrifice of a human victim. Kinsley observes, "Kālī reveals that ultimately all creatures are her children and also her food and that no social role or identity can remove the individual from this sacrificial give and take."[2] Often depicted as drinking blood from a skull bowl, Kālī's dietary preference for blood connects her symbolically with strength, vigor and life. Although she gives life as the Divine Mother, she also demands a continuous flow of fresh blood for subsistence in order to sustain her creative activity.[3] In other words, the cycle of life of which Kālī is the hub is indicative of the fact that life sustains itself on other life in a never ending cycle of death and life.

The sword of Kālī, the mad mistress of the universe, suggests the death of ignorance, whereas her girdle of severed hands indicate the end of grasping.[4] Or her sword can signify the mergence of all souls and their deeds in the Goddess.[5] Kālī's sword held high in a threatening position ready to strike the head of an unfortunate victim bears a remarkable similarity to the *vagina dentata* (vagina-with-teeth) that possesses the ability to castrate penetrating males. Since there is a connection between semen and the male head because of the belief that semen rises into and is stored in the head in Indian thought, especially in Tantric modes of belief, there is little distinction between beheading and castration.[6] The severed heads adorning her neck indicates the withdrawal of the mundane realm into the Goddess.[7] Her lolling tongue consumes not only blood, but all things, just as time *(kāla)* eventually consumes everything without social, economic and educational distinctions in its wake.[8] Her close association with time directly connects her with death, the dark sides of her divine nature and her symbolic color–black. When her devotee dies she can bestow release through her grace from the cycle of *saṃsāra* (rebirth). In a sense, Kālī tries to scare humans into rejecting the world, turning and surrendering to her.

Although Kālī gives human beings good reason to be fearful of her terrifying, awesome and frightening nature, she also manifests paradoxically a more loving aspect. Many of her images depict her upper right hand, her auspicious side, making the *mudra* (hand gesture) sign of "fear not," whereas her lower right hand makes the *mudra* sign of granting boons. To those who truly love her with all their being, she appears as the giving, life sustaining mother. But to those who neglect or reject her worship, she appears as a terrible shrew. Is this inter-

---

[2]David Kinsley, Hindu Goddesses: *Visions of the Divine Feminine in the Hindu Religious Tradition* (Berkeley: University of California Press, 1986), p. 130.

[3]Idem, *The Sword and the Flute,* p. 156.

[4]Ibid., p. 143

[5]C Mackenzie Brown, "Kālī, the Mad Mother," in *The Book of the Goddess Past and. Present: An Introduction to Her Religion,* ed. Carl Olson (New York: Crossroad Publishing Company, 1983), p. 116.

[6]O'Flaherty, p. 84.

[7]Brown, p. 116.

[8]Kinsley, *The Sword and the Flute,* p. 140.

pretation of Kālī's paradoxical nature foreign to Rāmakrishna's understanding of her nature?

Rāmakrishna recognized three aspects of Kālī: life-giver; life-sustainer; and destroyer. As the life-giver, she is worshiped in the ordinary Hindu household as the dispenser of boons and the dispeller of fear. During tragic periods of epidemic, famine, earthquake, drought or flood, she functioned as the sustainer and protectress. When the embodiment of the power of destruction Kālī appeared in her terrifying form.[9] But what about her dark appearance? Rāmakrishna was convinced that she appeared black to individuals because they viewed her from a distance, whereas those who truly knew and loved her did not perceive her as black.[10] For true devotees, she was colorless.

If one assumed that her temple image was an inert object, one falsely comprehends her manifestation. Since Rāmakrishna spoke, caressed, fed, dressed, joked, laughed and danced before her image, his behavior indicated a much different comprehension of it. In fact, her image was alive, as it appeared in some of his visions to be discussed later. In his study of the *Aśṭamīpūjā* to Durgā in Bengal, Östör refers to the *sandhi,* the final part of the ritual of union. He explains:

> Sandhi is the moment of the goddess's appearance. It is said that great devotees may see the goddess taking the form of her image, the image beginning to move, nodding her head, and giving blessings. In neighboring areas the goddess is said to leave footprints in a plate of vermillion dust at this time. But only those who are specially selected by the goddess can witness these things.[11]

Östör's observation is not only instructive, but it is also applicable to Rāmakrishna, who also conceived of the image of Kālī as alive. Thus the image of Kālī in the Dakshineswar temple was not an inanimate object. Therefore, Rāmakrishna could have a meaningful and intimate relationship with it. From a more philosophical perspective, Kālī is *śakti* (creative energy), like a gem and its brilliance or like milk and its whiteness.[12] *Vidyā* (knowledge) and *avidyā* (ignorance) are two aspects of this primal energy. The former leads to devotion, wisdom and the Goddess, the creative energy itself, whereas the latter leads to delusion and bondage.[13] As the creative energy of the universe, she is *prakṛti* (primal matter), the ever emerging stuff of creation composed of the three *guṇas (sattva, rajas* and *tamas).* The three *guṇas* constitute only the nature of *Śakti* and not Brahman, which is the impersonal absolute beyond the *guṇas.*[14] What is the rela-

---

[9]M, p. 135.

[10]Ibid., pp. 135, 271.

[11]Ákos Östör, *The Play of the Gods* (Chicago and London: University of Chicago Press, 1980), p. 83.

[12]M, p. 635.

[13]Ibid., p. 116.

[14]Ibid., p. 280.

tionship between Brahman and *Śakti* or Kālī? For Rāmakrishna, they form a unity: "'Brahman and Sakti are identical, like fire and its power to burn.'"[15] In order to emphasize the oneness of Brahman and *Śakti,* Rāmakrishna also used other analogies: "water and its wetness," and "the snake and its wriggling motion."[16] If we examine *Śakti* and Brahman from the perspective of action and inactivity, even though they are the same ultimate reality, Rāmakrishna elucidates that Brahman is inactive, whereas *Śakti* is the active aspect of the one reality which creates, preserves and destroys.[17] It is, for instance, like an ocean (Brahman) and its waves *(Śakti),* the moving, active aspect. Since *Śakti* is the active aspect, it forms the instrumental and material cause of the universe, like a spider (instrumental cause) makes its web from its own body (material cause).[18] Thus *Śakti* and Brahman are equally real, although Brahman possesses an ontological priority over the creative energy.[19] An important religious consequence of Rāmakrishna's position is that a *bhakta's* love for the Goddess, a personal deity, is not inferior to an individual's quest for knowledge of Brahman, an impersonal aspect of the one reality.

If Kālī represents the active, primal, creative energy of the universe and forms one reality with Brahman from a philosophical perspective, what sense can we make of her from a more religious viewpoint? Throughout Indian religious history, goddesses have played an important role in the religiosity of the people. The numerous goddesses of the Indian tradition can be classified into two or three major types depending on the scholarly authority that one chooses to consult. A goddess may adhere to the image of a cow, a terrifying figure, or the Pārvatī model,[20] or the typology can be simplified to two categories: goddess of the tooth or those of the breast.[21] The goddess of the breast or the good cow is a generous bestower of her life-giving fluids, auspicious, fertile, undemanding, passive and usually married. The breast goddess tends to overlap with the Pārvatī image, a benevolent, faithful and even obsequious wife.[22] The goddess of the tooth or the terrible figure is ambivalent, dangerous, vengeful, cruel, unpredictable and demonic. The terrifying goddess is usually unmarried, erotic and sometimes castrating, her immense power is to be feared. These fierce, aggressive and angry goddesses, like Kālī and Durgā, inflict punishment upon individuals in an often capricious manner, and it is impossible for mere mortals to control their energy or circumscribe their power. Even though Rāmakrishna acknowledged the more gruesome aspects of Kālī's nature, he would probably dis-

---

[15]Ibid., pp. 108, 134, 269.

[16]Ibid., p. 290.

[17]Ibid., pp. 283, 567, 634.

[18]Ibid., p. 835.

[19]Matchett, p. 174.

[20]Gananath Obeyesekere, *The Cult of the Goddess Pattini* (Chicago: University of Chicago Press, 1984), p. 440.

[21]O'Flaherty, pp. 90-91.

[22]For a comparison of the obsequious wife and. a more free feminine spirit see Olson, pp. 124-44.

agree with contemporary scholars. He would be tempted to place Kālī in the more benign cow or breast categories because she was for him the loving mother, although she could cause anguish in her devotee by withholding her presence.

Since Kālī controls everything and everyone, human beings cannot escape her control. Thus it is preferable to surrender to her power and do what she wants you to do.[23] Because Kālī–the universal mother–protects her children and grants their desires, Rāmakrishna became convinced, as his spiritual relationship to her deepened, that it was best to assume the attitude of a child towards its mother.[24] This attitude of Rāmakrishna has caused some scholars to interpret his behavior as a psychological regression to childhood and nonindividuality and a rejection, according to Zimmer,[25] of his manliness, individual achievement and exertion of ego. In a similar vain, Schneiderman interpreted Rāmakrishna's life by stating, "At first, he was like a child looking for his mother, seeking an improbable relationship with an image made of basalt, an inanimate and ferocious-looking mother-surrogate. It is striking that, even after Ramakrishna's real mother came to live at Dakshineswar permanently, he remained fixated on Kali."[26] The dramatic fantasy life lead by Rāmakrishna and the perception of Kālī's motherly nature coincided, according to Schneiderman, with his obsessive preoccupation with his own mother.[27] Without asserting that these types of scholarly approaches are totally incorrect, it can, however, be affirmed that these types of psychological reductionisms are without a firm foundation because they are based on mere conjectures. There is no direct textual evidence that Rāmakrishna was obsessed with his own mother. It is more hermeneutically productive to understand Rāmakrishna's attitude within his comprehension of play *(līlā)* discussed in the previous chapter and his manifestation of madness to be discussed in the next chapter. By playing the role of an innocent child, Rāmakrishna transformed a potentially dangerous Kālī into a loving mother figure. This is the innate power of the child; it can elicit the maternal instincts of the most horrible shrew.

In Hindu mythology the left side of Kālī, representing her ambiguous, destructive, dangerous and chaotic aspect, tends to predominate. There is, however, a tendency by Rāmakrishna to turn the ferocious Kālī into a more passive, limpid and nonthreatening figure. He tends to do this by not emphasizing her negative, terrible and dangerous aspect.

---

[23]M, p. 460.

[24]Ibid., pp. 141, 321, 381.

[25]Heinrich Zimmer, "Die Indische Weltmutter," *Eranos Jahrbuch,* 6 (1938), p. 213.

[26]Leo Schneiderman, "Ramakrishna: Personality and Social Factors in the Growth of a Religious Movement," *Journal for the Scientific Study of Religion,* 8 (Spring 1969), p. 69.

[27]Ibid., p. 69.

ATTITUDES TOWARD WOMEN

Since women participated in the sacrificial cult, performed their own sacrifices, became priests, were allowed to remarry, were not hindered from becoming scholars, teachers and poets and were permitted to be initiated *(upanayana)*, the Vedic period of Indian religious history was more liberal toward women than its later development. By the time that the *Manusmṛti* (ca. second century C. E.) was finally composed, the status of women was generally lowered and their creative freedom was restricted because they were prohibited, for instance, from the study of Vedic literature, reciting sacred *mantras* and the initiation rite. Although women were honored and respected as mothers and ideal wives *(pativratas)*, there have been historically many negative attitudes toward women in Indian literature. Women were subjected to seclusion *(purdah)* in the homes of the higher castes, socially pressured to commit *sati* (self-immolation) on their husband's funeral pyre and socially ostracized when they became widows. Because Rāmakrishna was a product of his culture, he inherited and espoused many of the negative attitudes toward women in general gained from his cultural heritage.

A frequent refrain uttered by Rāmakrishna was "women and gold" to summarize everything that is impermanent, the embodiment of ignorance *(avidyā)* and *māyā* (illusion).[28] M reported that Rāmakrishna stated that any monk who enjoyed the company of a women is akin to someone who swallows his own spittle after he has already expectorated.[29] There is evidence that women followers of the Master were segregated behind a screen when he gave instructions to everyone.[30] Rāmakrishna also held traditional views of the ideal married woman who experienced little lust and anger, slept little, served everyone, worked hard and exercised frugality. The ideal wife was also loving, kind, modest, devoted and helped her husband increase his love of god.[31] But why was Rāmakrishna's attitude toward women so negative overall?

In short, women led men away from the path of religion and robbed them of their spirituality.[32] Thus men must beware of the deceitful motives of women and be cautious about contact with them. Women could also prove a great danger to a world renouncer *(saṃnyāsin)* because he could lose his semen, which is believed to be very harmful. Therefore, it is best for a renouncer to live isolated from women even if a given woman is very religious.[33] Why is the loss of semen so important? Rāmakrishna's belief, like many Indian males, equated loss of semen with loss of spiritual power.[34] The renouncer must be careful not to even look at the picture of a woman because this could cause a nocturnal emis-

---

[28]M, pp . 82, 247, 439, 748.
[29]Ibid., p. 387.
[30]Saradananda, II: 803.
[31]M, pp. 701-02.
[32]Ibid., pp. 603, 387.
[33]Ibid., pp. 412, 184.
[34]Ibid., p. 411.

sion.[35] Thus it is important for a renouncer to observe strict discipline and avoid all women. In an autobiographical admission, Rāmakrishna told M that if he touched a woman his hand became numbed and ached.[36] This physiological reaction and revulsion to women suggests the Master's detached state and a latent misogynist attitude.

If it is recalled that Rāmakrishna was married, even though his marital union was never consummated, his expression to M that he was afraid of women is rather interesting. Although Rāmakrishna was able to alleviate some of his fears about women later in life, he reminisced about his early period with M confessing that he was very apprehensive about women to the extent that he imagined that they were ferocious, voracious felines coming to devour him. He also confessed that women impressed him as female monsters with prodigious bodies, limbs, and even the pores of their skin seemed large.[37]

This is a rather startling psychological admission by the Master, who is stating that he feared being devoured by women whom he called tigresses and she-monsters. Was Rāmakrishna fearful of having his penis devoured by the ferocious teeth of female monsters? This is a real possibility confirmed obliquely by Saradānanda's biography of the Master in which he reports two relevant episodes. Relating Rāmakrishna's physical reaction to the touch of lewd women, Saradānanda reports that his sexual organ would shrink instantaneously.[38] At another time, Rāmakrishna perceived the Divine Mother in some harlots and, again, he notes, "His sex-organ became contracted and entered completely into his body like the limb of a tortoise."[39] Saradānanda does not inform us how he acquired this knowledge about the extraordinary anatomical dexterity of Rāmakrishna's penis. Nonetheless, his sexual organ's unusual ability is consistent with his emphasis on renunciation, his admitting of adverse reactions to the touch of women and his fear of females. With this scenario in mind, the withdrawal reaction by his penis is perfectly consistent and even plausible, at least, in a metaphorical sense.

Reference was made above to the sword of Kālī that suggests a connection to the *vagina dentata* of male fantasy and fear. If we place Rāmakrishna's withdrawing penis within the context of Kālī's castrating sword, the reaction of his penis makes perfect sense because its withdrawal suggests a fear of castration. The primary problem for a male encountering a *vagina dentata* is to attempt to neutralize its dangerous power. A male could, if he were heroic enough, pull the teeth from the vagina or seize the sword in Rāmakrishna's case. This heroic act would transform the Goddess into a nonthreatening being. Rāmakrishna was not, however, heroic enough to try to break her teeth or capture her sword. He rather assumed the roles of a child, a female, or he withdrew his penis from danger. Although these were nonheroic responses, they were nonetheless effective.

---

[35]Ibid., p. 412.
[36]Ibid., p. 965.
[37]Ibid., p. 593.
[38]Saradananda, I: 773.
[39]Ibid., I: 199.

Besides Rāmakrishna's negative reaction to women, he also expressed a paradoxically positive view. Based upon what has been already stated, how was this possible? Rāmakrishna summarized his position, "'Women are, all of them, the veritable images of Sakti.'"[40] In other words, no matter how lowly a woman was, for instance, socially, she was still the image of Kālī, the Divine Mother. While riding in a carriage, Rāmakrishna saw two prostitutes standing on a verandah, appearing to him as the embodiment of Kālī, and saluted them.[41] After a performance at the Star Theater on Beadon Street in Calcutta, a few actresses, who were often of dubious virtue, came to the Master and saluted him by bowing before him and touching the ground with their foreheads. After some of them touched the Master's feet as part of their obsequious greeting, Rāmakrishna responded, "'Please don't do that, mother!'"[42] Conversely, virgins are also manifestations of the Goddess, and they should also be saluted and worshiped.[43] Regardless of a woman's sexual condition, whether harlot or virgin, all women are reflections of the Divine Mother because Kālī, as the *Ādyāśakti*, has assumed all female forms.[44]

For Rāmakrishna, then, all women receive their worth as manifestations of the Goddess, which is the reason he can also take a positive attitude toward them. If one should treat all women with respect because they are reflections of Kālī, what attitude should one assume with relation to them? Since all women can be regarded as his mother, the best attitude to assume, according to Rāmakrishna, is that of a child.[45] Thus Rāmakrishna did not decide to treat women as equals or as real persons. If one should assume the attitude of a child in one's relationship to all women, this represents the fabrication of a fantasy type of relationship grounded in the religious conviction that all women are representatives of Kālī on earth. Thus ordinary women become participants in the realm of play.

It appears that many women were willing to participate in Rāmakrishna's religious, playful, joyful fantasy. M reported that Rāmakrishna possessed many female devotees, although the Master did not discuss them very much with his male followers.[46] On the surface, this would seem to be contradictory or odd based on the Master's negative attitude toward women grounded historically in the Indian tradition. Why were women attracted to Rāmakrishna?

His conviction that all women reflected Kālī does not seem to be sufficient reason for his ability to attract female devotees, if we combine it with his general negative attitude. Manisha Roy offers us a plausible answer to our dilemma in understanding the attraction of Rāmakrishna to women of his time. In her work, she traces the life cycle of upper-class Bengali women from birth to mar-

---

[40]M, p. 116.
[41]Ibid., pp. 776, 284.
[42]Ibid., p. 683.
[43]Ibid., pp. 393, 168.
[44]Ibid., p. 701.
[45]Ibid., p. 377.
[46]Ibid., p. 804.

riage and into old age. The female informants tell Roy of idealized images of marriage which go unrealized and result in frustration. Feeling unwanted, worthless, and lonely later in life or when their husbands die, many of these women turn to a *guru*. Roy writes:

> For her emotional self, and this is usually unconscious, the *guru* may take the shape of a father whom she loved and adored in her childhood, a husband whom she expected to love and receive love from in her youth, and a brother-in-law and a son she is going to lose soon. And above all, the *guru* is the medium by which she can reach the god, the ultimate to which a mortal can aspire. The religious content that she was socialized to know as the underlying content of a husband-wife relationship (the model of Krishna and Rādhā as the acme of romantic as well as religious love) allows her to relate to her *guru* without any difficulty.[47]

A woman's chosen *guru* offers her an opportunity to be dependent and to be depended upon by someone. The *guru* also offers security, attention, pleasure, satisfaction, indirect sexual gratification by means of a woman's fantasy, emotional gratification and an opportunity to give of herself and receive recognition for it.[48] Since the scenario described by Roy has probably persisted for sometime, it is not unreasonable to surmise that a similar mechanism motivated women's attraction to Rāmakrishna.

RĀMAKRISHNA AND HIS WIFE

Having concluded the review of Rāmakrishna's attitude and relationship to women in general, it is now useful to investigate his relationship to a particular woman. Since the evidence about his relationship to his mother is sparse and unclear, it is best to look at the more abundant textural evidence about his relationship to his wife.

We know that Rāmakrishna married Sāradā Devī in May 1859, when he was around twenty-three and she was five years old. Soon after his marriage, and allegedly to appease his mother, Rāmakrishna returned to his priestly duties at Dakshineswar where his wife finally joined him when she was around thirteen years old. His biographers relate sentimental accounts of Rāmakrishna instructing his young wife in religious and domestic matters. What type of character did Rāmakrishna's wife possess?

According to the biography of Sāradā Devī composed by Swami Gambhirānanda after her death, she was kind, unpretentious, quiet, obedient, self-effacing, performed her duties meticulously, cared for the sick and served as a mother figure for young devotees at the temple. Like the goddess Śrī Lakshmī, the consort of Vishnu, Sāradā Devī played the role of the obsequious wife by massag-

---

[47]Manisha Roy, *Bengali Women* (Chicago and London: University of Chicago Press, 1975), p. 140.

[48]Ibid., p. 141.

ing her husband's feet, rubbing oil on his body and preparing nourishing and palatable meals according to his taste and delicate stomach.[49] Due to Rāmakrishna's assertion that the distinction between pure and impure was merely a product of one's mind, he insisted on her cooking for him while she had her menstrual period, a time when women are traditionally considered impure and potentially polluting.[50] The Master obviously enjoyed her care and attention for his comfort and welfare. Overall, Sāradā Devī is depicted by her biographer as a model wife.

It is acknowledged by her biographer that she was fundamentally an uneducated person, although she demonstrated an appreciation and enthusiasm for learning. Later in life she learned to read a little, but she could never even sign her name.[51] Her almost illiterate condition did not detract from her dignity and charm.[52] She suffered physically in her later years from rheumatism and a biliousness that produced a burning sensation over her body.[53] She also suffered mentally and emotionally from internecine family problems. Considering the importance of children to Indian women, Sāradā Devī also appeared to suffer from the unfulfilled desire to have children. Responding to the divisive talk of her friends and mother, Rāmakrishna told his wife that she would have so many children that she would be overburdened with caring for them.[54] Rāmakrishna obviously had his devotees in mind and proved to be prophetic.

There were periods in her life when she must have been very lonely. Her biographer refers to her not seeing her husband for periods of two and six months, even though they lived in close proximity.[55] Rāmakrishna was, of course, continually surrounded by devotees as his fame spread. And this may have also limited her access to her husband. On the other hand, she shared Rāmakrishna's bed with him at times. Her biographer makes clear that neither party desired any physical satisfaction. According to her biographer, their sharing of a bed was solely a spiritual experience.[56] This is an obvious justification for an espoused world-renouncer sleeping with his wife from the perspective of the biographer. Without drawing any perverse conclusions, it is reported that Sāradā Devī slept in the same bed with Yogin-Ma, a close, devoted, female friend after the death of her husband.[57] It is also important to observe that Sāradā Devī's attention to the Master was reciprocated by him, who often visited her cottage during the day and spent some time with her.[58] Although her biographer tried to depict her as the

---

[49]Swami Gambhirananda, *Holy Mother Shri Sarada Devi* (Madras: Sri Ramakrishna Math, 1955), p. 87.

[50]Ibid., p. 87.

[51]Ibid., pp. 30-31.

[52]Ibid., p. 497.

[53]Ibid., p. 501.

[54]Ibid., p. 126.

[55]Ibid., pp. 78, 80.

[56]Ibid., p. 47.

[57]Ibid., p. 112.

[58]Ibid., p. 64.

ideal wife and close companion of Rāmakrishna, there are hints that their relationship was far from exemplary. Periods of separation, isolation of his wife, frustrated child-bearing desires and possible lack of his wife's sexual satisfaction are factors contributing to a baffling interpersonal relationship. But, then, there are no guidelines for someone married to an incarnation *(avatāra)*.

If Rāmakrishna treated other women as manifestations of Kālī, one would expect to find the same attitude expressed towards his wife. The biographers make it clear that Rāmakrishna conceived of his wife as a living form of the Goddess.[59] As a manifestation of the Goddess, Rāmakrishna even worshiped his wife during a religious service. After sanctifying her with holy water and appropriate *mantras* (sacred formulas), both husband and wife entered *samādhi* (absorption) and became one.[60] In a sense, this represents a spiritual perfection of their marriage, which transcends any physical consummation. The biographer of Sāradā Devī is stating that their marriage is sacred, transcends any ordinary conjugal relationship and possesses cosmic significance.

PLAY AND THE FEMININE ATTITUDE

If women generally were considered mundane manifestations of Kālī, and if Rāmakrishna worshiped his own wife as an earthly form of the Goddess, what can we expect from the behavior of Rāmakrishna himself? In order to complete the feminine thread that runs through his life, Rāmakrishna assumed the appearance, behavior and attitude of an earthly and divine woman. Rāmakrishna usurped, however, the role of a woman not because of some perversion in his personality, but rather in the spirit of play.

While absorbed in a state of *samādhi*, Rāmakrishna's hands would mirror the hand gestures of a Kālī image.[61] These gestures gave hope and dispelled fear because they imitated the right or auspicious side of the Goddess. At other times, Rāmakrishna imitated a professional female singer, dressed like a woman,[62] or simply caricatured the actions of women to the delight and merriment of his male devotees.[63] He is reported to have worshiped Kālī dressed as a woman and became so absorbed in his feminine mood that he forgot about his male body.[64] One could interpret these actions as a manifestation of Rāmakrishna's confused sexual role. This may be partly true. We must, however, remember the religious context in which he lived his life. If we recall that all women are forms of Kālī, it makes perfect sense to imitate those closest to the Divine Mother of the universe. Kālī, the divine *Śakti*, casts her magical spell by means of her *yoga-māyā*, a force that enables her to perform play *(līlā)* in the world.[65] Only those with in-

---

[59]Ibid., p. 46; Saradananda, I: 333.
[60]Ibid., pp. 49-50.
[61]M, p. 928.
[62]Ibid., pp. 232, 603.
[63]Saradananda, I: 397-98.
[64]Ibid., I: 238.
[65]M, p. 533.

sight know her exercise of *yoga-māyā*. To the ignorant or indifferent, she appears as *māyā-Śakti,* a distorting and negative force.[66] Since Rāmakrishna possessed insight into the mysterious actions and nature of Kālī, he was free to enter into her *yoga-māyā* and play the part of a woman and revel in the company of the Goddess.

Rāmakrishna's emphasis on the motherly aspect of Kālī's nature suggests a nonerotic relationship with her. Nonetheless, their relationship takes place within a context of play *(līlā)*. In order to become a fully accepted participant in Kālī's game, it is advisable to become a female. The frolic of a male turned female alleviates unconscious male fears of an overpowering, threatening, mysterious, female figure. This especially makes sense, if we consider the male sexual anatomy with its exterior, visible and potentially erectable member, a situation that renders the male penis vulnerable to attack. By his ability to withdraw his penis into himself and assume the role of a female, Rāmakrishna's unconscious fears were dispelled and enabled him to play with and serve the Goddess without concern to his sexual anatomy.

Like the benign aspect of the Goddess that he worshiped, Rāmakrishna frequently assumed the role of a mother. Overcome by a feminine mood, an ecstatic Rāmakrishna placed his pillow on his lap, caressed it and held it to his breast as if he were nursing an infant.[67] He also played the role of a protective and nurturing mother toward, for example, Narendranāth his beloved disciple. He fed Narendranāth and stroked his disciple's body affectionately.[68] When his disciple did not visit for awhile Rāmakrishna became very concerned and inquired about his welfare. By playing the role of a mother, Rāmakrishna demonstrated that sex roles are transferable from one sex to another within the realm of play *(līlā)*, within which anything was possible. To assume the benign aspect of the Goddess also illustrates that Rāmakrishna understood his masculinity and feminine mood as two aspects of a single reality, which is reason enough for one to rejoice in the play of Kālī

It is not simply enough, however, to frolic as the handmaiden of the Goddess. The individual must also realize that Kālī dwells within the six centers of one's body.[69] The Goddess is thus present in the world and within the individual. Therefore, one can frolic outwardly with the Goddess in her realm of play and rejoice inwardly because of her internal presence.

Moreover, to usurp the feminine mood benefits one on the path to salvation. The feminine mood can help one conquer one's passions.[70] By assuming the nature of a woman before complete realization, this enables one to sport *(līlā)* with the Goddess.[71] Thus if a male is to enter fully into play, he must as-

---

[66]Wendy Doniger O'Flaherty, *Dreams, Illusion, and other Realities* (Chicago: University of Chicago Press, 1984), p. 300.

[67]M, p. 869.

[68]Ibid., pp. 768, 804.

[69]Ibid., p. 301.

[70]Ibid., pp. 176, 603.

[71]Ibid., p. 604.

sume the feminine mood. This is the thread that not only binds one to Kālī, but also unties one from the ropes of bondage and ties together one's life into a meaningful whole.

Chapter IV

MADNESS

While a priest in the temple at Dakshineswar, Rāmakrishna reached a point where he could no longer conduct the worship of the Goddess, just sitting inert before the stone image. He experienced wide mood swings. At one moment he would act like a demented person and the next moment he would cry profusely like a child.[1] Besides sitting immobile before the statue of Kālī, sometimes he would converse with the image as if it were alive and conscious. At other times, he brought food to the image and begged the Goddess to eat. With tottering steps, Rāmakrishna approached the Goddess, appearing to resemble a drunkard, endearingly touched the chin of the image, and commenced to talk, joke and laugh; he would even sing and dance holding the hands of the image.[2] Even though the Hindu devotional tradition considers divine images to be alive, Rāmakrishna's actions were still considered very strange by fellow Hindus. He gave the appearance to others of being mentally confused because he would lose all track of time during evening devotional services and forget to conclude the ceremony.[3]

As a priest in the Kālī temple, Rāmakrishna's behavior included some unorthodox practices: he would offer flowers to the Goddess after touching his feet with them; before offering food to the Goddess, he would eat the offerings; he would also lie in the bed of the Divine Mother.[4] On one occasion, after lower caste people were fed at the temple, Rāmakrishna took some of the leftover food off the leaf-plates and carried the food on his head to the bank of the Ganges. Then he swept the place with a broom and washed it with his own hands.[5] Anyone observed doing these ritually incorrect, religiously offensive and impure actions would be characterized as mad by an orthodox Hindu of the time. Based on his behavior in the temple, Mathur, business executive for the temple, concluded, for example, that Rāmakrishna was insane.[6]

From an objective perspective based on his biographies, Rāmakrishna appeared to be mentally confused about his own identity. On several occasions, he dressed, talked and behaved like a woman. And according to the accounts of other people, he was a very convincing female. At other times, he assumed the guise

[1]Life of Sri Rāmakrishna, p. 54.
[2]Ibid., p. 59.
[3]Ibid., p. 54.
[4]Ibid., p. 60.
[5]Saradananda, I: 159.
[6]Ibid., I: 188.

and demeanor of Hanumān, the monkey general of epic literature. Haladhari, a scholarly man employed by the temple, saw Rāmakrishna sitting naked on a branch of the banyan tree of the Panchavati, a grove of sacred trees used as a place of meditation, near the temple urinating.[7] While engaged in *kīrtana* with his devotees, Rāmakrishna was naked as he paced up and down the room, repeating the names of various deities.[8] Identity confusion and consistent aberrant behavior lead one to conclude that Rāmakrishna was a very disturbed person.

Besides overt forms of unusual behavior, Rāmakrishna often thought, or imagined, that he heard odd sounds and voices; and he also saw strange visions of divine beings. When Rāmakrishna sat to meditate, for instance, he heard strange clicking sounds in the joints of his legs. It was as if someone were locking his legs to render him motionless; and he heard the same sounds at the conclusion of his meditation, as if someone were unlocking his legs to free him.[9] Periodically, Rāmakrishna lost consciousness of the outer world and often had visions during these periods. After losing consciousness at one time, he proceeded to talk to the Goddess, chided her for the ostentatious display of her sari, told her not to bother him and to please be seated and be quiet.[10] On another occasion he went into *samādhi* when he heard a devotional song; his entire body became still, and he stood transfixed with his hand touching a plate of food.[11] Or his body became transfixed for long periods during a state of *samādhi* with his unblinking eyes wide open and his breath barely perceptible.[12] Just as suddenly as he had gone into a state of absorption, he returned to a normal state of consciousness. Rāmakrishna's penchant for drifting suddenly into trance states was also a manifestation of his wide mood swings. When he felt separated, for example, from the Goddess he wept profusely. Then he passed into a trance state, and he found Kālī standing before him smiling, talking and consoling him.[13]

Wide mood swings, memory lapses, sitting immobile, having conversations with no visible persons, laughing and dancing with an inanimate object, personal identity and sex-role confusion, hearing sounds and voices, apparent hallucinations in the form of various kinds of visions, and loss of normal consciousness are behavioral and psychological phenomena associated with Rāmakrishna, according to the Master himself and objective observers. What psychological sense can one make of these phenomena? Did Rāmakrishna suffer from an affective disorder? Or did he have schizophrenia?

The mental functions of someone suffering with an affective disorder (sometimes referred to as a manic-depressive disorder) are impaired to such a degree as to interfere with that individual's ability to function normally in society.[14] Wide

---

[7]Ibid., I: 188.

[8]M, p. 122.

[9]Swami Nikhilananda, "Introduction," in *The Gospel of Sri Rāmakrishna*, p. 14

[10]M, p. 319.

[11]Ibid., p. 182.

[12]Ibid., p. 175.

[13]Nikhilananda, p. 14.

[14]I have relied on the following works for my definitions of affective disorders and schizophrenia: American Psychiatric Association, *Diagnostic and Statistical Manual*

alterations of mood are most common in someone suffering from an affective disorder, which makes it difficult for that person to respond appropriately to common problems. In addition, such a person may demonstrate severe perceptual, language and memory deficiencies, which alter one's mental grasp of one's situation in life. A change in self-attitude might mean that a manic individual believes oneself to be God or possesses a secret knowledge to save humankind.With the examples of Rāmakrishna's actions already cited, one can acknowledge that he manifested some of these symptoms. But does this imply necessarily that he should be classified as having an affective disorder? Rāmakrishna's mental condition, mood alterations, changes in self-attitude and subjective sense of alteration in mental energy and bodily health were rooted in his religious enthusiasm. In fact, he was very cognizant of his mental and emotional condition. Speaking about himself, Rāmakrishna said, "'Again, he is like a madman. People notice his ways and actions and think of him as insane.'"[15] Thus Rāmakrishna was aware of his mental condition and actions, and he understood that others also perceived him as mad. Although Rāmakrishna manifested wide mood swings, memory lapses and perception deficiencies, he was well aware of his situation, even though he might not have been in total control of his condition.

Rāmakrishna's behavior was often bizarre, withdrawn, regressive, excitable, fearful, perplexed and confused, which are some of the symptoms often associated with schizophrenia. Besides corollary mood alterations, inappropriate emotional responses, loss of empathy (a symptom that does not apply to Rāmakrishna based on his concern for the welfare of others and love for them), reduction in spontaneous movements and activity (e.g., catatonic rigidity in Rāmakrishna's case), the schizophrenic's thought contents are altered to such a profound degree as to lead to misinterpretations of reality accompanied by delusions, a comprehension that one's thoughts, feelings or actions are not one's own but imposed by some external force, and hallucinations in either or both auditory and perceptual forms. Rāmakrishna also manifested a loss of ego boundaries, confusion about his own identity and sexual role, impaired work, withdrawal from the external world for periods of time, and preoccupation with fantasies. Although Rāmakrishna did have, for instance, visions, which one could term hallucinations and delusions, he was able to function with a modicum of success as a temple priest and religious instructor. Moreover, he understood his visions, which were frequently of divine beings, to be more real than his ordinary form of existence, a lesser reality or even considered unreal when compared to ultimate reality, Brahman.

Even if one assumes on the bases of the numerous examples given that Rāmakrishna was insane, his madness must still be placed within a Hindu religious context in order for it to make any sense. Within this context, Rāmakrishna did exhibit many symptoms associated with schizophrenia and af-

---

of Mental Disorders, Third Ed. (Washington, D.C: American Psychiatric Association, 1980) and Paul R. McHugh and Phillip R. Slavney, *The Perspectives of Psychiatry* (Baltimore and London: The Johns Hopkins University Press, 1983).

[15] M, p. 405.

fective disorder. But given the distance between the present moment and this late nineteenth century figure, it is difficult to determine with any accuracy from which disease he suffered.

In fact, Neevel thinks that Rāmakrishna was able to overcome his insanity. Neevel attempts to prove his point by contending that the healing and mental transforming factor was Rāmakrishna's Tantric realization that the entire world is filled with only God.[16] Thus Neevel argues that Rāmakrishna was transformed from a madman in his early years into a saintly teacher in his later years.[17] This assertion is incorrect because of contrary evidence. With the assistance of Bhairavi Brāhmani, a wandering Tantric ascetic from a Brahmin family of the Jessore district of Bengal, Rāmakrishna experientially realized the ultimate truth of Tantra around 1863-64. If one recalls that Rāmakrishna died on August 15, 1886, there is a gap of approximately thirteen years between his Tantric realization and his death. If Neevel is correct, there should be no evidence of his madness during this thirteen year period, but this is not the case. In fact, Rāmakrishna continued to drift into *samadhī,* which from one perspective represents a lapse of worldly consciousness and withdrawal from others. His alternating states of ecstasy were punctuated with long periods of perfect lucidity and intimate interpersonal relationships when he instructed his followers and others. On July 31, 1885, M reported the following words of the Master:

> 'Formerly I too used to see many visions, but now in my ecstatic state I don't see so many. I am gradually getting over my feminine nature. I feel nowadays more like a man. Therefore, I control my emotion; I don't manifest it outwardly so much.'[18]

Rāmakrishna spoke these words approximately one year before he died. These confessional words indicate that Rāmakrishna was not yet totally cured of his madness, rather he was on his way to recovery. Although he continued to drift into ecstatic states, the visions that accompanied them were becoming less frequent. Furthermore, his sex-role confusion was "gradually" being cured, and he was becoming less confused and more certain of his male sexuality.

Due to the fact that Rāmakrishna died in 1886 and is obviously no longer available for a personal interview, it is extremely difficult, if not impossible, to diagnose his mental illness with any accuracy. It seems best to leave psycho-history to someone like Erik H. Erickson and to avoid conjecture. Another danger is the possibility of reducing Rāmakrishna to some convenient or, for that matter, even appropriate diagnostic category and fail to take him very seriously as a religious figure of consequence. By following an earlier suggestion, it seems wiser to place Rāmakrishna and his madness within his religious context because there is a long tradition of religious madness in India. This procedure will enhance one's chances of understanding the meaning of his madness.

---

[16]Neevel, p. 78.
[17]Ibid., p. 53.
[18]M, p. 798.

Rather than a clinically technical definition of madness, this chapter proposes to follow a more humanistic approach, like the descriptive and interpretative approach of an historian of religion. For someone to be perceived mad, that person must act continuously abnormal, which implies that he/she must act contrary to accepted norms of behavior or what people expect of a normal and mentally healthy individual. To deviate from the decorum of a temple priest in this case means that one runs the risk of being labelled crazy. For someone to lack consistent intention, to act outrageously, to appear indifferent to what one says and does, and to behave in an unpredictable manner are characteristics of a mad person. With this general definition of madness as our guide, we will place Rāmakrishna within his religious tradition and attempt to elucidate the religious significance of his madness.

HINDU RELIGIOUS TRADITION OF MADNESS

Krishna, Śiva, Rāma and Kālī were some of the deities significant in the life of Rāmakrishna, who manifested madness by their unusual behavior or appearance in the Hindu religious tradition.[19] These divine beings and others had the ability to inspire a similar madness in their devotees.

Within the Vaiṣṇava tradition, for instance, Nammāḷvār, the ninth-century, gifted poet-saint and most eminent of the twelve Āḷvārs (ones immersed in god),[20] travelled to southern India reciting his poetic creations about his god, his agonizing search for his deity and the pain of separation from his beloved. Nammāḷvār's spiritual odyssey drove him mad at times:

> Mumbling and prattling
>   the many names
>   of our lord of the hill
> with cool waterfalls
>   long strands of water,
> while onlookers say,
>   "They're crazy,"
> entering and not entering
>   cities,
> standing still or swaying
>   before a laughing world,
> they dance, they leap,
>   undone by feeling—
> and the gods bow down
>   before them.[21]

---

[19] See David Kinsley, "'Through the Looking Glass:' Divine Madness in the Hindu Religious Tradition," *History of Religions*, Vol. 13, No. 3 (May 1974), pp. 271-286.

[20] A. K. Ramanujan, "Introduction," in *Hymns for the Drowning: Poems for Viṣṇu by Nammāḷvār* (Princeton: Princeton University Press, 1981), p. ix.

[21] Ibid., p. 54.

Sober members of society thought that the poet was a demon, an idiot, or mad *(pēy, pittaṉ)* due to his god-intoxicated condition. But the poet stood emotionally naked before an amused world because he could not control his intense feelings. A later Āḻvār poet named Kulacēkaran acknowledged that the *bhakta* (devotee) was mad and appeared crazy to others. What accounts for this madness? An insightful observation is made by Hardy: "The 'madness' of religious ecstasy is the human response to the madness implied in Kṛṣṇa's *māyā:* ideal bhakti is 'madness,' and only by means of it can something of the gulf created between the *bhakta* and Kṛṣṇa by the latter's *māyā* be bridged."[22]

During the late thirteenth century in western India, Guṇḍam Rauḷ, the second major *guru* of the Mahānubhāva sect, manifested very unorthodox behavior. Known popularly as Gosāvī, he, for example, went into a home and broke the storage pots and mixed food together.[23] He often acted infantile, greedy, rude, excessively demanding and petulant. Gosāvī frolicked in his madness. While a devotee combed his hair, she discovered a louse which she then gave to him. Gosāvī slapped the louse and either threw it away or placed it somewhere else in his hair.[24] His behavior was very unpredictable and sometimes included the stealing of food, a manifestation of his obsession for food. This was rather strange behavior for someone believed to be an incarnation of the sect's one god, Parameśvara (supreme lord).

The thread of madness continued in the Vaiṣṇava tradition in the fifteenth century with Mīrābāī (1403-70), allegedly a Rājput princess who refused to commit *sati* (self-immolation on her husband's funeral pyre) after her husband died.[25] Rejecting her former socio-economic status, widowhood and former husband, she accepted Krishna as her true husband and lover. She wrote that the intoxicating sound of Krishna's flute has driven her mad.[26] Her separation from her beloved and her subsequent profuse sufferings also contributed to her madness,[27] as confirmed by normal members of society.[28] Mad with love, unable to control her senses, and the personal property of god, Mīrābāī wrote in the Rājasthānī dialect of Hindi:

> But I am just a poor mad girl.
> An arrow from the quiver of love

---

[22]Friedhelm Hardy, *Viraha-Bhakti: The Early History of Kṛṣṇa Devotion in South India* (Delhi: Oxford University Press, 1983), p. 434.

[23]Feldhaus, 278.

[24]Ibid., 80.

[25]See S. M. Pandey, "Mīrābāī and Her Contributions to the Bhakti Movement," *History of Religions,* Vol. 5, No. 1 (Summer 1965), pp. 54-73.

[26]A. J. Alston, trans., *The Devotional Poems of Mīrābāī* (Delhi: Motilal Banarsidass, 1980), 167, 80.

[27]Ibid., 97.

[28]Ibid., 36, 37.

Has pierced my heart and
driven me crazy.[29]

Unable to control her feelings, she was at the mercy of her emotions and deity.

The experience of separation from one's deity and the agony caused by such an existential situation has been a common theme of the Hindu devotional tradition. We encounter the theme of separation again in the life of Caitanya, the sixteenth- century Bengali saint. Caitanya experienced uninterrupted consciousness of separation from Krishna day and night, a condition that drove him mad.[30] Caitanya experienced wide mood swings and incoherent behavior. He would laugh one moment and cry the next. He would dance, run swiftly to and fro, and suddenly fall down faint upon the ground. His physique gave symptomatic signs of his madness: his limbs would grow stiff, tremble, his skin would perspire profusely and appear to change color, and his hair would stand on end.[31] Besides his mental and physical disorientation, his senses were also confused, and he spoke nonsensically with his beloved deity.[32] By reciting religious verses, his followers tried to calm him at night when his anguish grew worse.

Caitanya's feeling of separation from Krishna made him think of his god even more intensely. He relates that he repeated his beloved's name incessantly, while his mind became unhinged, prompting him to laugh, weep, sing and dance ecstatically.[33] He imagined that he saw Krishna everywhere. As he came from the ocean one day, he spied Caṭaka Mountain which he imagined to be the mythical Govardhana, a mountain held aloft by Krishna to protect the *gopīs* from a tremendous storm created by a jealous Indra, and ran towards it.[34] Caitanya's emotional and mental absorption in Krishna ecstasy was sometimes dangerous because he almost drowned in one episode when he jumped into the ocean to play with his deity; he had mistaken the ocean for the Jumna River of idyllic Vṛndāvana where Krishna stole the clothing of the *gopīs*.[35] Caitanya's mind was never far from heavenly Vṛndāvana where he might be transported unconsciously; a flower garden might remind him of Krishna's paradise, causing him to weep, wildly searching for his beloved and reciting religious verses.[36] As Kennedy remarked in an earlier biography of his life and movement, Caitanya remained throughout his life a "minstrel of Hari, with a song in his heart and the lilt of it ever upon his lips."[37] If the blue ocean or a flower garden reminded him

---

[29]Ibid., 38.

[30]*Caitanya-caritāmṛta of Kṛṣṇadāsa Kavirāja, edited with the commentary Gaurākṛpa-taraṅgiri by Rādhāgovinda Nath,* 6 Vols. (Calcutta: Bhakti-pracana-bhaden, 1949-50), II.2.2-6; III.6.4-5; hereafter cited as C. C.

[31]Ibid., II.2.63; III.14.85-89.

[32]Ibid., II.2.4-5.

[33]Ibid., I.7.74-75.

[34]Ibid., III.14.79-80.

[35]Ibid., III.18.30.

[36]Ibid., III.15.28-29.

[37]Melville T. Kennedy, *The Chaitanya Movement: A Study of the Vaishavism of Bengal* (Calcutta: Association Press, 1925), p. 55.

of his god or something associated with his deity, the blue neck of a peacock and the sound of a flute would send him into an ecstatic trance.[38] On the one hand, Caitanya was obviously not at home in the mundane world where he could hardly function as a fully responsible adult. On the other hand, his madness allowed him to function at another level of truth.[39]

The madness of Caitanya is carried on by the later Bāuls of Bengal. Wandering minstrels of Bengal, the Bāuls subsisted on the meager earnings from their singing and the charity of their listeners. Driven mad by the sound of Krishna's flute, they adorned themselves in rags and cast-off clothing. "The Bāul is thought mad because he goes deliberately and powerfully against the current of custom."[40] An observation that can be accurately applied to other mad *bhakti* devotees.

In the Mahārashtra region of India during the seventeenth century, Tukārāma, a devotional poet and mystic, was born into a poor family; he assumed the family business after his older brother became a *saṃnyāsin* (world-renouncer). After a brief period of prosperity and happiness, Tukārāma's life was shattered by business failure and a series of family deaths. Upon renouncing the world, he retired to a mountain and eventually received a vision of Krishna, whose effect was to make him mad.[41] In a poem he acknowledged, "I am changed from a sane man to a mad man."[42] The symptoms of his madness are very similar to those experienced by Caitanya: "My hair stands erect, sweat breaks forth upon me; a flood of tears fills my eyes; my eight limbs are filled with thy love. I will consume all my body in uttering thy praises; I will sing thy name day and night."[43] And like Caitanya, he continually performed *kīrtana* in public. Tukārāma's younger wife and shrew—Avalī—thought that he was crazy.[44] Her opinion was shared by the local people who reasoned that Tukārāma was crazy because he danced in the temple and repeated the names of god day and night.[45] The experience of separation from god was also present in Tukārāma's case,

---

[38]C. C., II.17.204; II.18.151-52.

[39]Edward C. Dimock, "Religious Biography in India: The 'Nectar of the Acts' of Caitanya," in *The Biographical Process: Studies in the History and Psychology of Religion*, eds. Frank E. Reynolds and Donald Capps (The Hague: Mouton, 1976), p. 113.

[40]Idem, *The Place of the Hidden Moon: Erotic Mysticism in the Vaiṣṇava-Sahajiyā Cult of Bengal* (Chicago: University of Chicago Press, 1966), p. 251.

[41]R. D. Ranade, *Mysticism in India: The Poet-Saints of Maharashtra* (Albany: State University of New York Press, 1983; reprint of *Indian Mysticism: Mysticism in Maharashtra*, 1933), p. 303.

[42]J. Nelson Fraser and K. B. Marathe, ed. & trans., *The Poems of Tukārāma*, 3 Vols. (Madras: The Christian Literature Society, 1909, 1913, 1915), 361, 1408.

[43]Ibid., 749.

[44]Justin E. Abbott, trans., *Life of Tukaram translation from Mahipati's Bhaktalilamrita, Chapters 25 to 40* (Delhi: Motilal Banarsidass, 1980; reprint of First Ed., 1930), 28; 33; 30.88; 31.64; 33.81.

[45]Ibid., 29.57-58; 31.20.

which merely increased his madness.[46] He was mad with desire and passion for his beloved, which made him consciously oblivious to the world.[47] Thus he could not function in society like a normal human and assume responsibilities. Besides being incapable of providing for his family, at least according to his nagging wife, Tukārāma could not hold a job or perform simple duties. While hired to guard a farmer's grainfield, for instance, he let the birds eat all the seeds.[48] Waiting for god to reveal himself, Tukārāma barked and growled in a fit of madness.[49] In short, he had been transformed into a mad dog.

If we turn to the Śaiva tradition, we discover madness among the Pāśupatas, worshipers of Śiva as the Lord of Beasts. Historically, the Pāśupatas were probably Brāhmanical theists following the *Śvetasvatara Upaniṣad*. In their theology, creatures *(paśus)* are bound to the world by the fetter (*pāsa*, meaning cause and effect) of ignorance, a beginingless state of bondage from which one sought escape. Their path of liberation shared similarities to other yogic disciplines, for example, celibacy, detachment from worldly objects, withdrawal of the senses and concentration. Their conviction that the acquisition of good karma was necessary in order to construct a superhuman body, which would eventually equate them with Śiva, motivated them to practice some unusual procedures. A *pasu* (creature) should live in or near cremation grounds in order to more easily bath three times a day in ashes, a means of purification of one's body, thought and self. The ascetic should go naked or clothe oneself in a single cloth. At a later stage in the ascetic path one should act mad or ridiculous in order to incur the censure of members of society, thereby cancelling one's bad karma and transferring the merit of others to oneself.[50] Rejecting any sectarian marks on one's body, one must act the madman by suddenly falling down trembling, making believe that one was asleep, acting epileptic, limping, speaking nonsense, playing the role of a lecher, laughing, covering one's body with filth, letting one's beard, nails and hair grow long. In short, the Pāśupatas wanted to imitate and transform themselves into the Lord of Beasts himself.[51]

Other Śaiva ascetic movements manifested madness. The Kālāmukhas, for instance, followed the thought of the Pāśupatas in the Karnātaka region of India from the eleventh to the thirteenth centuries by bathing in ashes and carrying a staff.[52] They ate from a skull bowl and worshiped with a pot of wine. In a similar fashion, the Kāpālikas,[53] whose origins date from around the seventh century, carried a human skull from which they ate their meals, smeared their bodies with ashes and carried a trident *(khatvānga)*. Besides also using wine in their worship,

---

46 Fraser and Marathe, 785.

47 Ibid., 785, 1283.

48 Abbott, 28.70-89.

49 Fraser and Marathe, 1376.

50 Daniel H. H. Ingalls, "Cynics and Pāśupatas: The Seeking of Dishonor," *Harvard Theological Review*, Vol. LV (1962), p. 291.

51 Ibid., p. 295.

52

53 See David N. Lorenzen, *The Kāpālikas and Kālāmukhas: Two Lost Śaivite Sects* (Berkeley: University of California Press, 1972).

they allegedly engaged in human sacrifice by means of self-mutilation using pieces of their flesh as sacrificial offerings. The madness of their spiritual discipline also included alleged licentious sexual behavior. A much less sanguine type of Śaivism is found in other aspects of the tradition.

After the appearance of the hymn singing, sixty-three Nāyaṇārs whose works are contained in the *Tirumurai* anthology and the *Tevāram*, a collection of devotional hymns by the poets Sambandar, Appar and Sundarar, the Śaiva poetic tradition reached its culmination with the *Tiruvāsagam* of Māṇikkavācakar of the ninth century.[54] The great poet was converted by Śiva's grace, which melted his soul and dispelled his sins.[55] The theme of separation was again evident in his poems. Māṇikkavācakar thought that god had forsaken him.[56] Since he could not live apart from Śiva, the poet asked god to reveal himself. Seeking his beloved, Māṇikkavācakar wandered around "raving."[57] Just as Caitanya's strange behavior was often triggered by a sight of something associated in his imagination with his god, when Māṇikkavācakar saw the golden hall of the Naṭarāja temple at Cidambaram he was transported into ecstasy, and the temple guard thought that he was crazy.[58]

Śiva, the ocean of grace and mercy, was considered mad by Māṇikkavācakar. The ruler of the universe and dweller within human souls appeared mad to the south Indian poet because he wore animal skins, snakes, ashes, skulls, bones and the matted hair of an ascetic. Thus Śiva was a mad god who drove his devotee crazy waiting for the gift of love, freedom from the fetters of past karma and impurity of mind, and union (conceived as a marital love) with Śiva.

After Śiva revealed himself to the poet in the form of a *guru*, we catch a glimpse of the symptoms of madness similar to those already noted with Caitanya and Tukārāma of the Vaiṣṇava tradition. Māṇikkavācakar wrote about crying, repeatedly shouting, confusion, falling and rolling on the ground and bewilderment.[59] For Māṇikkavācakar, to become intoxicated with Śiva entailed becoming crazy, a madness of love. Since the poet was transformed into a madman, he was now like the mad deity who possessed him. Unfettered by reason, egoism, social relations, and the structures of mundane reality, the poet stood unconditioned in his absolute freedom.[60] Although he had become a madman, Māṇikkavācakar had been totally transformed by the grace of his deity.

Similar to the world renunciation by Mīrābāī of the Vaiṣṇava tradition, Mahādēviyakka, a Vīraśaiva female saint of the twelfth century, also renounced her husband (unlike Mīrābāī her spouse was alive) and betrothed herself to Śiva.

---

[54] Ibid., chapters 2-3.

[55] For an argument about this date see Glenn E. Yocum, *Hymns to the Dancing Śiva: A Study of Maṇikkavācakar's Tiruvācakam* (Columbia, MO: South Asia Books, 1982), pp. 46-50.

[56] G. U. Pope, trans., *The Tiruvāsagam of Mānikka-Vāsagar* (Oxford: Clarendon Press, 1900), 8.79-82.

[57] Ibid., 6.23.90.

[58] Ibid., 41.3.10.

[59] Yocum, p. 53.

[60] Pope, 3.150-55.

Some have concluded that she had married a Jain king called Kausika. The *Śūnyasaṁpadane*, however, recorded that she was not married to a king, but had left her native village.[61] She refers to her spiritual marital status in the following way: "Linga the bridegroom, I the bride."[62] In another poem, she wrote:

> Cennamallikārjuna is my groom:
> All other husbands in the world
> Are naught to me![63]

Thus the beautiful lord of white jasmine was her lawful husband in her mind.[64] Besides her earthly husband, she also renounced her parents and clothing, wandering around the countryside covered only by her hair. Her nakedness and wandering life-style were symbolic of her total freedom and rejection of the world, which she referred to as, for example, "illusion's chamberpot," "passion's whorehouse," and a "leaky basement."[65]

Although Śiva was her adopted husband, she was driven mad by their separation. She wrote poetically, "Four parts of the night/I'm mad for you."[66] When her spiritual husband was absent she grew lean from loss of appetite. Even though their separation caused physical and psychological problems for Mahādēviyakka, it had erotic benefits:

> Better than meeting
> and mating all the time
> is the pleasure of mating once
> after being far apart.[67]

For Mahādēviyakka, it was not a matter of the quantity of sex; but she was more concerned with the quality of sexual intercourse with her erotic and ascetic deity.

MADNESS AND THE DIVINE

In the initial chapter of this book, reference was made to the eclectic nature of Rāmakrishna's religiosity, a characteristic that is manifested in his saintly madness. By successfully experimenting with different Hindu paths to liberation (e.g., Tantra, Vedānta, and *bhakti*) and practicing Islam and Christianity for brief

---

61 Yocum, p. 185; See also Glenn Yocum, "'Madness' and Devotion in Māṇikkavācakar's Tiruvācakam," in *Experiencing Śiva: Encounters with a Hindu Deity*, eds. Fred W. Clothey and J. Bruce Long (New Delhi: Manohar, 1983), pp. 19-36.

62 S. S. Bhoosnurmath and Armando Menezes, trans. *Śūnyasaṁpādane*, Vol. IV (Dharwar: Karnatak University, 1970), p. 262.

63 Ibid., p. 296.

64 Ibid., p. 302.

65 A. K. Ramanujan, trans. *Speaking of Śiva* (Baltimore: Penguin Books Inc., 1973), p. 111.

66 Ibid., p. 133.

67 Ibid., p. 124.

periods, Rāmakrishna manifests from one perspective possible religious confusion. Orthodox representatives of Hinduism, Islam, or Christianity might view Rāmakrishna's experiments as a form of madness. Unlike previous Hindu religious figures mentioned above who were mad for their chosen deity and expressed their madness in language and/or behavior, Rāmakrishna was uniquely mad for a variety of Hindu deities, a feature of Rāmakrishna's behavior grounded in his conviction that all sects and religions are really many paths to the same goal.

Rāmakrishna demonstrated madness, for instance, towards Krishna. Sometimes, he imagined himself to be a *gopī* (milk maid) of Vṛndāvana gone mad over the beauty of Krishna, singing improvised songs of his devotional feelings and seeing Krishna in all things and everywhere.[68] At other times, he thought of himself as Rādhā longing for her beloved. To a follower who was convinced that madness was undesirable, Rāmakrishna explained that the madness of Rādhā was not over worldly things. Rather the origin of madness was due to meditating on god, resulting in love-madness and knowledge-madness.[69]

There were strange physiological results of his devotion to Krishna: a burning sensation in his body; an oozing of blood from the pores of his body; a loosening of bodily joints; and a cessation of his sense faculties and physiological functions.[70] As Rāmakrishna lay motionless and unconscious, he resembled a dead man, a necessary condition for spiritual rebirth.

As a devotee of Rāma, Rāmakrishna assumed the role and attitude of Hanumān by eating only fruits and roots, living in trees, jumping from place to place instead of walking, and tying a cloth around his waist and letting it hang down to form a tail. Rāmakrishna proudly reported that his coccyx enlarged by about an inch.[71] Rāmakrishna was also mad for Rāmalāla, the boy Rāma. He carried a brass image of Rāmalāla with him, bathed it, fed it and laid it down to sleep.[72] Since these actions represented a form of *pūjā* (a series of devotional acts of service or respect to a deity as a royal guest), this could be called *pūjā* madness because of the extremes to which Rāmakrishna went in his devotion. But why was this type of activity significant? Just as Sītā was madly in love with Rāma, Rāmakrishna said, "'One must become mad with love in order to realize God.'"[73] Thus even a common devotional practice like *pūjā* must be done overzealously.

A good example of the extremes to which devotional madness can drive the devotee was the confession of Rāmakrishna that when he experienced divine madness he would worship his own penis as a substitute for the *liṅga* of Śiva,[74] the erotic and ascetic deity. Unfortunately, Rāmakrishna does not relate to us whether his penis was erect or limp when he performed this act of devotion. This

---

[68]Ibid., p. 140.
[69]M, p. 212.
[70]Ibid., p. 220.
[71]Saradananda, I:272; Nikhilananda, p. 25.
[72]*Life of Sri Rāmakrishna*, p. 63.
[73]M, p. 346.
[74]Ibid., p. 346.

is a question raised not by prurient interest but because of Rāmakrishna's unconsummated marriage and extremely negative sexual attitudes.

As noted earlier, some of the most intense manifestations of Rāmakrishna's madness were connected to his adoration of Kālī, the Black One. Without a constant experience of the Goddess by means of visions or feeling absorbed in her, Rāmakrishna was filled with a poignant sense of separation, which was overtly exhibited when he threw himself violently on the ground, cut his face by rubbing it on the ground, wailed loudly and almost ceased breathing. His entire body was covered with blood from the cuts and bruises that were self-inflicted.[75] Due to his agony of separation from his beloved Goddess, Rāmakrishna decided that life was empty, meaningless and no sense living. Thus Rāmakrishna decided to commit suicide in order to be freed from his emotional and mental anguish. While coming to this drastic decision within the temple of the Goddess, Rāmakrishna spied suddenly the sword held by the image. When the madman ran to seize hold of the sword, he had abruptly a wonderful vision of his beloved one and fell unconscious to the temple floor.[76] Thus his madness is grounded in his religious quest for what he perceived to be the truth.

An important episode within the overall scenario of Rāmakrishna's madness occurred one day in the temple, while he was preparing to offer food to the image of Kālī, a part of his customary duties as a temple priest. Instead of offering the food to the Kālī image, Rāmakrishna saw a cat and blasphemously fed it with the offerings intended for the Goddess. The manager of the temple garden was outraged by Rāmakrishna's mad behavior and reported this incident to Mathur. What motivated Rāmakrishna to perform such an insane and blasphemous act? He gave as his reason that he had become aware that Kālī had become everything in the universe--including the cat.[77] From his perspective, Rāmakrishna was not feeding a cat, but he was rather directly offering food to Kālī. Thus Rāmakrishna's madness allowed him to perceive everything as the Goddess. The madness of Rāmakrishna enabled him to gain a positive insight into the nature of reality. From a religious perspective, Rāmakrishna's madness was not a distortion or confusion about the nature of reality, but it represented rather a revelation about the true nature of reality.

Since Rāmakrishna's intense, all-consuming—mental, physical and emotional—quest to personally experience and become absorbed in these various divine beings motivated him to do bizarre things, one cannot simply assume that his eclectic search for religious certainty caused his madness, although it may have contributed to it. His madness may also have been caused by his partial or complete loss of self. When one's mind becomes annihilated on the path to ultimate knowledge the ego also disappears, and one enters *samādhi*.[78] The psychiatrist R. D. Laing recognizes that transcendental experience involves ego loss, a phenomenon also associated with madness.[79] If one retains a trace of ego, one

---

[75]Ibid., p. 491.

[76]Saradananda, I:174.

[77]Ibid., I:162.

[78]M, p. 346.

[79]Ibid., pp. 776, 169.

must accept, according to Rāmakrishna, the deity as a person with attributes.[80] Rāmakrishna refers to the ego in both negative and positive senses. On the one hand, the ego blocks the realization of ultimate reality and the ability to see the true nature of the divine.[81] A trace of ego, on the other hand, is a positive thing because it allows one an opportunity to enjoy the deity and to act as its servant.[82] Rāmakrishna's religious experiences do not appear to confirm the opinion of R. D. Laing. If transcendental experience and madness commonly share the loss of ego, it is possible that transcendental experience, according to Laing's argument, may contribute to the experience of madness. But this is not the case in India, where the loss of the self is essential for enlightenment.[83] Rāmakrishna wanted to retain a trace of self in order to engage in the playful madness of Kālī.

Mad saints and mystics are to be found in other religious traditions. In Islam, there was Abū Yazīd al-Bistāmī (d. 874), who once told a pilgrim on the way to Mecca to circle him instead seven times[84] and kissed a skull which he found and alleged that it symbolized Sufi annihilation *(fanā)*[85] and al Hallāj (d. 922), a famous Sufi martyr. Both Sufis claimed blasphemously in their own way to be God. Symeon of Emesa, an ascetic in the Eastern Orthodox Christian tradition who lived on wild herbs and roots, wore little clothing and resided under the open sky, also had little regard for decency because he wandered about naked, entered the women's bath and relieved himself in public. A story claimed that he dragged the carcass of a dead dog through the streets.[86]

---

[80]See R. D. Laing, *The Politics of Experience* (New York: Pantheon Books, 1967); *The Divided Self* (London: Tavistock, 1959); *The Self and Others* (London: Tavistock, 1961).

[81]M, p. 636.

[82]Ibid., pp. 385, 678.

[83]Ibid., pp. 280, 678, 788.

[84]O'Flaherty, *Dreams*, p. 121.

[85]A. J. Arberry, trans., *Muslim Saints and Mystics* (Chicago: University of Chicago Press, 1966), p. 114.

[86]Alexander Y. Syrkin, "On the Behavior of the 'Fool for Christ's Sake,'" *History of Religions*, Vol. 22, No. 2 (November 1982), pp. 153, 156. Beginning with its roots in the words of the apostle Paul and New Testament sayings of Jesus, John Saward in his work entitled *Perfect Fools: Folly for Christ's Sake in Catholic and Orthodox Spirituality* (Oxford: Oxford University Press, 1980) traces the historical development of the holy fool from the Eastern Orthodox tradition through the Middle Ages of the Western church, the Cistercians, its zenith in the fifteenth and early sixteenth centuries in such figures as Thomas More (d. 1535) and Philip Neri (d. 1595), the influence of St. Ignatius Loyola (d. 1556) and especially Père Lallemant (d. 1701) on such figures as Jean-Joseph Surin and others, and concludes with modern fools like Edward Bouverie Pusey (d. 1882) and the Irish holy man Matt Talbot in the twentieth century. Saward perceives the following characteristics of the holy fool in Eastern Christianity and to a less conspicuous degree in the Western Church tradition: (1) Christocentric inspiration for their identity and actions; (2) folly for Christ's sake is a charisma or gift from God; (3) simulated character of foolishness means that the fool plays at being mad; (4) eschatological because the fool proclaims a conflict between the present and future worlds; (5) pilgrimage for a promised land, which

In comparison to the madness of Rāmakrishna, a colorful madman of medieval Japanese religious history was Ikkyū Sōjun (1394-1481), who was allegedly the illegitimate child of Emperor Gokomatsu. After having attained full enlightenment *(satori)*, Ikkyū's erratic and bizarre behavior began to manifest itself as he bore the burden of preserving the authentic Zen tradition. This wanton madman called himself "Crazy-cloud." Since Ikkyū was a Zen monk, he was expected to keep his distance from women, a prohibition he could not accept. Ikkyū spied a woman with her skirt up, while he was crossing a river; he stopped to make three reverential bows toward her sexual parts.[87] Unlike Rāmakrishna, Ikkyū indulged himself fully in the sensuous pleasures of the world and committed acts that were contrary to monastic regulations. Besides his fondness for wine, he was a frequent visitor at local brothels. Ikkyū admitted in an autobiographical poem to "Racing back and forth from brothel to wine shop."[88] In order to discover the nature of the world's delusions, the *bodhisattva* (enlightened being) had to come into direct contact with them and experience them. To live in solitude within the walls of a monastery was to reside in a state of ignorance. Ikkyū's bizarre antics were a form of instructive pedagogy (*upāya*, skill-in-means). Brandishing a long, genuine looking sword with an elegant hilt and scabbard, Ikkyū played the role of a warrior in the streets of Sakai. When people stopped him to indicate that a sword was the proper possession of a warrior not of a monk, he would withdraw his fake sword to reveal its true nature, which resembled false wisdom.[89]

St. Francis of Assisi (1182-1266) was, like Ikkyū and Rāmakrishna, deemed mad by others. He was scoffed at as a madman and driven away with stones and mud thrown at him by kinsfolk.[90] At times, he was an emaciated figure clothed in rags with a cord for a belt, or he was seen preaching naked.[91] As a young man, he renounced the world and his father's wealth in front of Santa Maria Maggiore, the site of the episcopal palace, by tearing off his clothes and throwing them at his father's feet. When he read his rule before Pope Innocent III, he was told by the pontiff to find a herd of pigs to roll in the mud with. After fol-

---

implies that the fool is always a stranger and nomad; (6) political; (7) discernment of spirits; (8) fools are ascetics; (9) solidarity with social outcasts; (10) child like nature suggests a purity and simplicity of heart (pp. 25-30). Among the various forms of holy folly, Saward finds that the common denominator is the fool's enthusiasm for God (p. 216). Many of the Christian fools that Saward discusses were considered mad by their contemporaries. Hence apparent madness is another characteristic of the fool in the Christian tradition, although Saward does not develop this feature of the Christian fool in his book. The madness, foolish behavior, playfulness, playing the role of a stranger (as we will see in chapter six), ascetic demeanor, child like simplicity are all characteristics that Rāmakrishna shares with many of the Christian fools.

[87]James Sanford, *Zen-Man Ikkyū* (Chico, CA: Scholars Press, 1981), p. 283.

[88]Ibid., p. 131.

[89]Ibid., p. 38.

[90]W. Heywood, trans. *The Little Flowers of the Glorious Messer St. Francis and of His Friars,* Second Edition (London: Methven & Co., Ltd., 1924), p. 2.

[91]Ibid., p. 84.

lowing the Pope's instructions, he returned to the head of the church in a foul-smelling condition.[92] The madness of St. Francis was indicative of his divine, intoxicated condition, like the numerous Hindu saints already noted, and love of poverty in an attempt to imitate the life of Jesus.

MADNESS, WORLD AND INTERRELATIONSHIP

The world is, according to Rāmakrishna, like a thorny bush in which the more one struggles to free oneself the more one becomes entangled in its labyrinth of thorns.[93] Or one can imagine the world as a gigantic fishing net in which human beings—the fish—get caught. The fisherwomen is Kālī, whose *māyā* created this fishing net. Only a few fish escape the net, and many of the remaining fish captured in the net are not even aware that they are entangled and thus do not attempt to free themselves.[94] Whether one imagines being entangled in a thorny bush or a fishing net, to be immersed in worldliness is to be in a state of bondage. Rāmakrishna often used a short formula to express a being's immersion in worldliness, which he called "women and gold." The overwhelming majority of humans are mad for the things of the world, but this type of madness is, according to Rāmakrishna, misguided. In fact, Rāmakrishna's reaction to worldliness was rather bizarre. Rāmakrishna demonstrated dramatically to Dr. Bhagavan Rudra and others what happens to him when he simply touches a coin. After a devotee gave him a rupee, Rāmakrishna held it in his hand, and he began to wither in pain and his breathing also stopped. When the coin was removed from his hand, he returned to normal to the wonder of the confounded doctor.[95] This strange demonstration indicates that Rāmakrishna's madness was not of this world; it had a transcendent quality. If the things of the world are nothing more than an alluring trap designed to entangle human beings, how should individuals live in the world? Rāmakrishna's advice was to live in the world as the mudfish exists in mud. What does this mean for human beings trapped in the world? It suggests that in order to develop love towards the Goddess one must renounce the world and seek solitude for a period of meditating on the Divine Feminine. Afterwards, one is better prepared to live detached from the world, while one resides within it. Although the mud (world) is there and fish (humans) must live within it, one's detachment from the world implies that one is not stained by its mud. According to Rāmakrishna, it is thus possible for someone to lead the life of an average householder in the spirit of detachment and not fear the allurements of the world for one's spiritual welfare.[96] Or one should live like an ant. Since the world contains a mixture of sugar and sand (a metaphor for truth and falsehood), the ant takes the sugar and leaves the sand.[97] Besides being a mixture of truth and untruth, the world is best comprehended as a madhouse of

---

[92]Ibid., p. 96.
[93]M, p. 96.
[94]Ibid., pp. 164-65.
[95]Ibid., p. 845.
[96]Ibid., p. 336.
[97]Ibid., p. 472.

the Divine Mother.[98] This implies that in order for one to survive one must become mad. Since the world is created through the *māyā* (creative illusion) of the Goddess, it is unreal, ephemeral and a mere magic show. Thus it is foolish to be mad for the things of the world, which are merely transitory and like a dream. If one must be mad in order to feel safe within this madhouse, one should not be mad for the impermanent things of the world. If one must be mad, be mad for Kālī alone.[99] Rāmakrishna's message is to become mad for that which is permanent, ever-lasting and an ocean of immortality. To plunge into this ocean brings one immortal life and victory over death.[100] By becoming mad for the Goddess, we do not lose. To become mad for Kālī is risky because one must venture one's entire being, but the gamble of one's sanity enables one to win the all. Within the context of Rāmakrishna's thought, madness is a divine gift freely given by the Goddess to the adventurous risk taker.

Within this madhouse of a world ruled by the mistress of madness, one encounters other beings who are ensnared by the world's allurements. How can one help these unfortunate creatures? Rāmakrishna chose to teach and manifest his madness for Kālī and other deities in order to serve as a model for liberation.

However, other caring individuals misconstrued the madness of Rāmakrishna. Concerned about Rāmakrishna's mental health, Rani Rasmani and Mathur concluded that his problem might be due to his rigid observance of sexual continence. They thought that a break from his celibate regimen would be beneficial to his health. Therefore, they hired two prostitutes to provide the necessary cure. When the two harlots entered his room to tempt him, Rāmakrishna ran to seek shelter at the feet of Kālī,[101] a manifestation of Rāmakrishna's conviction to seek refuge in that which is permanent and not what is transitory. In another episode, Chandra Devi, the mother of the Master, became concerned about reports of her son's strange behavior and mental condition. Thus she assumed that marriage would help restore his mental stability.[102] Although a mate was found for Rāmakrishna, the marriage was never consummated probably because of Rāmakrishna's attitude towards the dangers of sexual intercourse for one's spiritual development and his apparent conviction that his real wife was Kālī. Another alleged incident in Rāmakrishna's life demonstrates the consistency of his anti-sexual attitude. An apparently insane woman, a spiritual aspirant who perceived god as her beloved sweetheart, came to visit the Master and identified him as her heart's delight. When she made her lascivious thoughts known to Rāmakrishna, he threw a violent child-like fit by jumping up from his seat in protest. As he rose from his seat, his loin cloth fell to the floor, giving the scene a comic twist, and he paced the room like a madman, cursing such an illicit relationship in the most vehement terms.[103]

---

[98]Ibid., pp. 516, 623.

[99]Ibid., p. 449.

[100]Ibid., p. 456.

[101]*Life of Sri Rāmakrishna*, p. 68.

[102]Ibid., p. 78.

[103]Gambhirananda, p. 127.

As observed earlier, numerous people who encountered Rāmakrishna concluded by their observations of his conduct that he was mad. None who encountered Rāmakrishna was more important historically than Narendranāth, later to be known as Swami Vivekānanda. After a *kīrtana* performance, Rāmakrishna took Narendranāth aside, and suddenly grasped the young man's hand as the Master shed tears profusely. With tears of joy running down his cheeks, the Master stood, folded his palms and paid homage to Narendranāth. Rāmakrishna told the young man that Narendranāth was in reality an incarnation of the ancient *rishi* Nara, a part of Nārāyana (Vishnu) himself, who had come to remove the misery and suffering of humankind. Narendranāth reported his reaction of this scene to Saradānanda: "'I was absolutely nonplussed and thought, Whom have I come to see? He is, I see, completely insane.'"[104] If Narendranāth was absolutely convinced that Rāmakrishna was mad, why did he continue to visit the holy, mad man? Two reasons can be conjecturally offered: Narendranāth was attracted to what he perceived to be the presence of the holy, and he found the madness of the Master irresistible and contagious. In other words, Rāmakrishna's madness functioned as a magnet to bring others closer to him and the locus of holiness that he represented. Thus his madness had an interrelational and unifying quality. For instance, while Narendranāth sang to the accompaniment of musical instruments one evening, a strange transformation occurred among the assembled devotees. Captured in a spirit of divine ecstasy, they became a mass of mad devotees, creating an electric atmosphere in which everyone felt the presence of the holy.[105] This unusual scene captures the spirit of Rāmakrishna's madness and its contagious nature.

In contrast to the interrelationships in Rāmakrishna's life, Ikkyū was very critical of the Rinzai leaders and the decadent Zen of his time, having deviated from the true spirit and practice of its eminent predecessors. Ikkyū's freedom and madness placed him outside the confining structure of the world and the social patterns of society. Unwilling to adhere to Zen monastic norms, Ikkyū's radical freedom based on his madness allowed him to enter into an illicit love affair with Mori, a blind singer, having initially met her when he was seventy-seven years old. He was also free to give a funeral for a dead cat, and paraded through the streets of Kyoto waving a human skull which was attached to the end of a long bamboo pole. This latter, bizarre gesture was his way of wishing others best wishes for the coming year.[106] The skull was a symbol for those who were spiritually dead.

MADNESS, MEANING AND PLAY

In his informative and insightful article on madness among Hindu saints, Kinsley enumerates five fundamental meanings of their madness. Kinsley thinks that the madness of Hindu saints indicates their total absorption in the divine.[107]

---

[104]Saradananda, II:825.
[105]M, p. 884.
[106]Sanford, pp. 93-94.
[107]Kinsley, "Divine Madness," p. 297.

The madness of the Hindu saint, often a sign of divine grace, suggests his/her participation in, or imitation of, the god or goddess that one adores.[108] Kinsley affirms that the madness of the Hindu saint marks him/her as someone who has renounced, or is indifferent to the world.[109] "The madness of the saints, fourth, suggests that they are not at home in the phenomenal world."[110] Finally, madness of the mad saints is a mark of their freedom and transcendence.[111] These interpretative points are certainly applicable to Rāmakrishna. Thus I do not want to dispute Kinsley's interpretation with which I essentially agree. However, I want to touch on some additional points pertinent to the madness of Rāmakrishna.

Mentally healthy people do not intentionally seek to gain madness. Normal individuals not only seek to avoid insanity, but they also pity those suffering from mental illness. In contrast to this general scenario, there is the biographical accounts of Rāmakrishna's radical request to Kālī to make him mad.[112] Why would he beg the Goddess for madness? Is this not itself an insane request? Within the context of Rāmakrishna's religious presuppositions, his radical request for madness makes sense because one cannot directly realize the Goddess through reasoning or rational arguments based on scripture.

By asking the Goddess to make him mad, Rāmakrishna is also requesting her to play with him. In other words, Rāmakrishna wants to become the mad toy of the Mistress of Madness. This request implies that Kālī will be in control, which motivates Rāmakrishna to imagine such connections between himself and his Goddess as being a machine of which she is the operator, being a house of which she is the interior resident, and being a chariot of which she is the charioteer. Rāmakrishna admits that he moves as she moves him, and when he speaks she speaks through him. Due to the degeneracy of the present *Kaliyuga*, it is impossible to hear the voice of the Goddess, which is the reason why it is necessary for her to communication through the mouth and being of a madman.[113] Since the world is a madhouse controlled by a mad Goddess in this final, degenerate and immoral age, those unfortunate individuals entangled and suffering within the world are potentially responsible only to the call of a madman. Thus all of the bizarre actions of Rāmakrishna, the divine plaything, are effacious in the Hindu context and a direct result of the playfulness of the Goddess, playing the game of madness on the stage of the world through her chosen, devoted and willing instrument.

Although others acknowledged Rāmakrishna's madness, as he did himself, the source of his insanity is not due to some organic mental disorder, affective disorder, dissociative disorder, psychosexual disorder, or personality disorder. It is grounded in the madness of the Goddess. Trying to explain his bizarre antics to Dr. Sarkar, Rāmakrishna said, "'All this is the result of my divine madness.

108Ibid., p. 298.
109Ibid., p. 300.
110Ibid., p. 301.
111Ibid., p. 303.
112M, pp. 295, 527.
113Ibid., pp. 616, 245.

How can I help it?'"[114] Rāmakrishna acknowledges that he is not only insane, but that he cannot control himself because he is an instrument—the mere plaything—of a greater power.

The mad Goddess of the universe touched Rāmakrishna and made him mad. In turn, Rāmakrishna touches human beings and drives them insane. For instance, after Rāmakrishna touched numerous devotees in a state of divine consciousness, their mood altered and some began to laugh, weep, meditate, call aloud to others to join them enjoy the grace of the Master and behaved like madmen.[115] Just as the Goddess played the game of madness with Rāmakrishna, he also played briefly with his followers by giving them the divine gift of madness, a manifestation of his compassion of those entangled and suffering in the world.

The madness of Rāmakrishna, like other ascetics and saints before him, functions as a symbol of the holy person, the divine-intoxicated one, the realizer of ultimate reality, or the liberated one. By personally experiencing ultimate reality, one may demonstrate wide mood swings, behave like a child, become inert and unable to work, experience visions, laugh, dance and sing in a mad frenzy. These symptoms of madness are a sure sign that such a person is a realizer of the Goddess. Furthermore, these symptoms of insanity are an indication that this life represents one's final birth.[116] The mad individual is no longer subject to the cycle of time. In this sense, Rāmakrishna's madness is a celebration of his freedom and a manifestation of it.

Unsnared by the world, unencumbered by society, and unbound by priestly decorum, Rāmakrishna can act mad in total freedom. Rāmakrishna is a mental and social misfit, whose radical freedom breaks down all order and points to the absurdities of conventional social life. His total freedom is accompanied by transcendence of phenomenal dichotomies, which implies that he does not differentiate, for example, between pure and impure.

Not unlike Rāmakrishna, Ikkyū was a social misfit, who demonstrated contempt for social and monastic status in Japan. He played the role of a warrior by carrying a wooden sword, played the role of lover and arrogated the dignity of a monk. When invited to perform an eye-opening ceremony (a means of giving life to a statue by painting in its eyes) for a new statue of the *bodhisattva* Jizo at Seki, Ikkyū climbed the ladder to the statue, while the people excitedly awaited the important religious event, and stood before the image and proceeded to urinate on Jizo's head to the utter astonishment of those assembled.[117] These are all examples of his playfulness, which he entered voluntarily without any deity's invitation. He sought to create disorder rather than order common to ordinary play. His play manifested his transcendence of earthly dichotomies and absolute freedom.

In Nietzsche's work the *Gay Science*, a madman runs to the market place in the early morning with a lantern in his hand seeking God. The populace laughs

---

[114]Ibid., p. 905.

[115]Saradananda, I:450.

[116]M, p. 783.

[117]Sanford, pp. 291-95.

at his antics, and they pay no attention to his announcement that God is dead. The lantern, thrown on the ground, broken and symbolically extinguished, leaves the madman to acknowledge that he had come too soon. In contrast, Rāmakrishna arrives at the most opportune time for his followers. His light and playfulness were not extinguished.

Chapter V

HUMOR

Is it true or false to argue that religious matters are serious business? Are not religious leaders or divinely inspired individuals expected to be serious? Are not spiritual liberation and bondage serious concerns to everyone? Would one not consider a religious leader with an acute sense of humor flippant or worse? Many people would probably answer these questions affirmatively. What needs to be recognized is that seriousness forms the foundation for humor, a profound expression of one's humanity, one's concern, one's insight into life situations, and one's playful nature. But are not most holy individuals or acknowledged living incarnations serious types of persons? This is not necessarily true, and Rāmakrishna confirms my observation by his behavior.

Unlike the Jesus figure presented by the writers of the Synoptic Gospels,[1] when reading M's account of the behavior of Rāmakrishna one is struck by his wonderful sense of humor, skill at telling jokes and funny stories, and delight of his laughter. His keen sense of humor is enjoyed by his followers who find his laughter contagious.

Humor and its concomitant laughter, according to Rāmakrishna, have a divine origin. The Goddess possesses a sense of humor, and she laughs on two occasions. She laughs when a physician claims to a patient's mother that he can cure the youngster. The Goddess is amused at the folly of the physician who falsely thinks that he is the master of the boy's fate and forgets to acknowledge that the Goddess is in control of life and death. The Goddess also laughs when two brothers divide their land, mutually agree on what belongs to whom, and forget that the entire world is the dominion of the Goddess.[2] Since the Goddess is the source of humor, she bestows it upon human beings as a gracious gift. In Hinduism gifts represent a form of sharing. Thus it is quite acceptable for one to share humor and laugh with Kālī. According to Rāmakrishna, Kālī talked with him after she arose from the Ganges River while Rāmakrishna was sitting under a banyan tree. Their conversation ended in a mutually shared laughter. Although

---

[1]See Elton Trueblood, *The Humor of Christ* (New York: Harper & Row, Publishers, 1964).

[2]M, pp. 105-06.

Rāmakrishna does not tell us what was so funny, he does say that it was a form of play.[3]

Rāmakrishna's sense of humor lacked sarcasm, which tends to be derisive, farcical and slapstick, which is often boisterous action. More often directed at incongruous persons or situations, Rāmakrishna's humor was also often directed at himself, a manifestation of his ability to laugh at himself. While eating from a basket of sweets brought by a devotee, Rāmakrishna said with a smile, "'You see, I chant the name of the Divine Mother; so I get all these good things to eat.'"[4] Again, he admitted to his devoted followers that he can eat a little fish soup in his current mental state, if the dish had been offered initially to the Goddess. He is forbidden, however, to eat any meat, even if it was offered first to the Goddess; but he acknowledged to his followers that he tasted meat with the end of his finger, even though he did not want to get her angry.[5] Rāmakrishna could also laugh when a ruse had been played on him, and even though he was suffering with cancer of the throat. For instance, an actress had been praised by Rāmakrishna for her portrayal of the young Caitanya, the famous Bengali saint, during his visit to the Star Theater in 1884. After learning of Rāmakrishna's illness, the actress, having become a devotee of the Master, was determined to visit him. Unable to simply visit the ailing Master because actresses were equated with prostitutes in the popular imagination in those days, she sought the assistance of another devotee, who disguised her as a male in European clothes and brought her to the Master. Gaining easy access to Rāmakrishna's room, the male devotee informed the Master about the true identity of the disguised actress at which Rāmakrishna laughed heartily. After praising her for her courage and devotion, Rāmakrishna gave her some spiritual instruction and allowed her to render devoted obeisance to him by giving her the opportunity to touch his feet with her forehead. With great enjoyment and relish, Rāmakrishna related to his disciples the trick that the actress had played on him, even though he was in constant pain caused by his cancer.[6]

According to his biographers, Rāmakrishna related to his devotees the origin of his smile and the cause of his laughter. At one point in his life, Rāmakrishna imitated the behavior of Hanumān, the monkey general of an army of monkeys and bears and devoted servant of Rāma of the epic *Rāmāyaṇa*. After meditating on Hanumān, Rāmakrishna's movements and way of life began to resemble those of a monkey by living on fruits and nuts, tying a cloth around his waist, a portion of it hanging like a tail, and jumping from place to place. By assuming the guise of Hanumān, Rāmakrishna was granted a vision of Sītā, the divine consort of the heroic Rāma, who entered his body and disappeared saying that she bestowed unto him her smile.[7] Rāmakrishna explained the cause of his laughter to his assembled devotees by relating the story of a man who fed a peacock a dossage of opuim at four o'clock in the afternoon, an action that caused the in-

[3]Ibid., p. 830.
[4]Ibid., p. 175.
[5]Ibid., p. 131.
[6]Isherwood, p. 299.
[7]Nikhilananda, p. 16.

toxicated bird to return at the exact time the next day to receive another portion of the drug. [8] This humorous story was told after M had entered the Master's room. Rāmakrishna laughed aloud and said that he had come again. The point of Rāmakrishna's remarks was that M was the peacock in the story returning for another dose of divine, intoxicated love from the Master. This episode also illustrated that Rāmakrishna's laughter derived from the joy he received from his devoted followers and that his laughter was something relational and something to be shared with others in their common search for religious salvation. Laughter cannot be quantified, it cannot be the sole possession of any one person, and it cannot be stored. It must be shared with others because it was, too, plentiful and overflowed any container— human or objective—that tried to contain it.

Since humor was such an important feature of Rāmakrishna's nature, this chapter will examine its nature, the variety of humor manifested by Rāmakrishna, its relationship to freedom, cohesiveness, and its dangers. This will afford us another opportunity to examine another form of play.

THE NATURE OF HUMOR

The comic *(hāsya)* sentiment is recognized in the *Nāṭyaśāstra*, the archetypical book of Indian drama, of Bharāta, the work's alleged author, as one of the eight legitimate sentiments.[9] Even though the erotic *(sṛṅgāra)* sentiment gives birth to the comic,[10] the latter is rooted in the durable psychological state of laughter, created by odd dress, strange talk, defective bodily appearance and human faults and follies. An individual can laugh alone, a form of the self-centered comic sentiment, or one can produce laughter in other people, the second type of comic sentiment that is centered in others.[11] That which is comic gives rise to laughter, which can be sublime or descend into vulgarity. Bhārata recognizes a hierarchy of laughter from the most refined to the most crass.

According to the *Nāṭyaśāstra*, there are six types of laughter: a slight smile *(smita)* without the teeth visible, which represents the refined manner of a superior, restrained person; a smile *(hasita)* that only slightly reveals the teeth; gentle laughter *(vihasita)* reveals a joyful, broad smile; a wider smile and more vigorous laugh *(upahasita)* manifests ridicule; vulgar laughter *(apahasita)* brings tears to the eyes and violent shoulder and head shaking; and excessive laughter *(atihasita)*, the most crass, vulgar, degrading, raucous and violent bodily form of laughter.[12] Laughter, a response to what one finds to be humorous, is not only a manner of the mouth, but it also involves one's eyes, nose and entire body. How one laughs indicates one's aesthetic taste, social refinement, caste standing, moral development, maturity and spiritual development.

The *Nāṭyaśāstra* does not give us a fully developed theory of humor, although it does provide us rather with a skeletal like framework by means of its

---

[8]M, p. 90.
[9]*Nāṭyaśāstra*, 6.15.
[10]Ibid., 6.39.
[11]Ibid., 6.48.
[12]Ibid., 6.52-59.

suggestions upon which we can build. Rather than intending to offer a fully developed theory of humor, a task which would need considerable space and is beyond the scope of this work, in order to supplement the classical Indian text, I only want to discuss some significant features that have relevance for this chapter.

In our everyday life, our normal day tends to follow a pattern that we have experienced before and expect to experience in the future. Our daily routine, our relationship to others and our general expectations about life fall into an orderly pattern, assuming that one is mentally healthy and normal. Breaks, interruptions and incongruous situations caused by a life crisis, like a death, divorce, loss of occupation, an odd event, an unusual saying or viewing something very strange can provide a disruption in our daily pattern that can lead to a response, for instance, on our part of anxiety, wonder or laughter. If our given conceptual pattern of understanding is jolted or our common perception altered, these disruptions can cause laughter when we respond to the incongruities of life. Rāmakrishna recognized this tendency in human beings with the following anecdote:

> In Burdwan I once saw an ox moving about the cows. I asked a bullock-cart driver: 'What is this? An ox? How strange!' He said to me: 'True, sir. But it was castrated in old age, and so it hasn't altogether shaken off the old tendencies.'[13]

Much like the castrated ox of Rāmakrishna's story, humans are also creatures of habit.

Perceived incongruity by an individual is not the sole cause of laughter. An unbearable tragedy in one's life can prompt hysterical laughter. A sadist may laugh at the misfortune of his/her victim and find pleasure in the suffering of an unfortunate person. Laughter can be dangerous in the sense that it can be arrogant, scornful, scurrilous, taunting and a tool of oppression, which reinforces our sexual, racist or ethnic prejudices and sense of superiority.[14] A tense situation or a life-threatening situation can cause one to accumulate nervous energy which may be released when the danger passes by a laughter of relief. Or one may respond to getting a job promotion, winning money, getting a book published or some other good fortune with laughter. Thus not all laughter is caused by humor or perceived incongruity.

Within the context of humor, one demonstrates to oneself and others that one is amused and enjoys a joke or funny anecdote. When one finds something amusing one discovers something unusual or odd, not necessarily in an objective sense. Even though one might often view something as incongruous and thereby funny in the objective world, what is humorous is the intentional object of thought cognitively perceived as incongruous. Thus what causes us to respond with laughter can be objective or subjective.

---

[13]M, p. 709.

[14]Conrad Hyers, *The Comic Vision and the Christian Faith: A Celebration of Life and Laughter* (New York: Pilgrim Press, 1981), p. 27.

What one perceives to be humorous is not merely determined by one's intellectual reaction to that which is incongruous, unexpected or illogical. Laughter involves, as John Morreall makes lucid,[15] a change of one's psychological state, which can be primarily cognitive, a change from seriousness to a nonserious condition of amusement, or an affective change, a cessation of negative feelings, a release of suppressed emotions or a rise in positive feelings. Rāmakrishna was able, for instance, to effect a change in a follower by asking whether or not he observed that the Master did not accept any monetary or other material gifts. Since no collection is taken at Rāmakrishna's residence, that is the reason so many people visit.[16] The change of our cognitive or affective conditions can be sudden and accompanied by a pleasant psychological change, a conceptual shift.

If our daily social intercourse entails predictable actions on our part and expected patterns of behavior by others, the conceptual shift caused by perceiving something incongruous and viewing it as humorous violates our pattern of daily expectations, which causes us to be surprised and even amused. What we assumed a thing, person or situation to be in fact is discovered by us not to be the case. In fact, our assumptions were incorrect. What we anticipated to be one way was really totally different. Rāmakrishna illustrates this with the following anecdote: A devotee of the Goddess worshipped her by sacrificing goats for many years before he suddenly stopped the practice. When a friend asked him why he stopped making sacrifices to the Goddess, the former sacrificer replied that his teeth had fallen out and that he had lost his ability to chew goat-meat.[17] The violation of our conceptual system, our daily safety net, is thrown askew, and we are caught off-guard, surprised, shocked about our assumptions and moved off our existential center. We laugh at the newly perceived incongruity of a person, thing or situation, and we may find that we enjoy the incongruity. The violation of our conceptual system and the concomitant conceptual shift when confronted with incongruity is necessary for humor, even though we need not enjoy our emotional shift.[18] Usually to respond to the conceptual shift with laughter indicates that we enjoy the newly perceived incongruity. The change can alter our conceptual system, and open us to other forms of novelty, as well as free us from the bonds of our anxiety.

When we discover what is odd or when we perceive humorous incongruity in common things, persons or situations, we celebrate our location in the world, and we come to know what it means to be without place. Our celebration and displacement enable us to thereby learn the meaning of place. By dislocating us, humor reveals place and what it means to be.[19] To be displaced by humor does not involve anything negative. On the contrary, humor gives us hope to cope with the anxieties of our existence; it leads us to encounter the other in dialogue.

---

[15]John Morreall, *Taking Laughter Seriously* (Albany: State University of New York Press, 1983), p. 39.

[16]M, p. 903.

[17]Ibid., p. 912.

[18]Morreall, p. 47.

[19]Harold Alderman, "The Place of Comedy," *Man and World: An International Philosophical Review*, Vol. 10 (1977), p. 169.

And humor returns us to our conceptual system with a new sense of place, others and ourselves. Thus humor can help us enjoy, relax and renew our energies. If humor returns us to our common world renewed, it refreshes us. Thus humor is not an escape from the world nor a fleeing from our moral and social responsibilities. Our recalcitrant attitude to change, our normal patterns of thought and behavior are severed, and we can become more accepting and ready to celebrate the unordinary or the strange within the ordinary.

TYPES OF HUMOR

If one tries to differentiate and classify the various examples of humorous behavior and sayings of Rāmakrishna, one finds a wide variety which can be categorized into four distinct types following the typology provided by Morreall.[20] The initial type of humor includes deficiencies of various kinds. A common form of incongruity is perceived in an object or person, like a dilapidated car, a misshapen object of some sort, or a human with a deformity, such as Quasimodo, Victor Hugo's hunchback of Notre Dame. Rāmakrishna used human deficiencies to make a humorous point in the following story: "'Once a blind man bathed in the Ganges and as a result was freed from his sins. But his blindness remained all the same.'"[21] At another time, Rāmakrishna related that a world-renouncer who associates with women and wealth is like a beautiful woman with a bad case of body odor. Just as the renouncer indulging in pleasure can never acheive his goal, the foul odor of the woman negates her beauty.[22] When Rāmakrishna laughs at something or someone his laughter should not be necessarily mistaken for ridicule. As a comedian, Rāmakrishna does not assume the position of a superior person speaking to or about an inferior individual. He is not, for instance, a learned Brahmin caste member, teaching an unlearned, lower caste person. Nor does he necessarily scurrilously ridicule an unfortunate person with a physical flaw because Rāmakrishna's humor is grounded in his love of the Goddess and other human beings.

Besides physical malformities, another kind of human deficiency is ignorance or plain stupidity. The gullibility of the pious masses is made clear by Rāmakrishna when he tells the story of a goldsmith whose tongue suddenly turned up and stuck to the palate of his mouth. Because the goldsmith became completely inert for a long time, others perceived him as a man absorbed in *samādhi* and began to worship him as a holy man. After several years, his tongue resumed its normal position, he regained consciousness of things in the world, and he thus returned to his original form of work.[23] Another humorous anecdote concerns Gauri of Indesh, a scholar, bigoted worshiper of Śakti and hater of anything associated with Vishnu, who used to pick up tulsi-leaves, items sacred to Vishnu, with a couple of sticks in order not to touch them with

---

[20]Morreall, pp. 64ff.
[21]M, p. 276.
[22]Ibid., p. 442.
[23]Ibid., p. 285.

his fingers.[24] Although it is true that absurd individuals or situations can be hilarious and pure nonsense can make one laugh, the humorously absurd and nonsensical does not necessarily make us evaluate ourselves and our actions. Rāmakrishna's humorous stories are often intended to make one engage in self-evaluation and self-examination, which tends to make his humor slightly less playful and more purposeful. Of course, Rāmakrishna's humor is also very often purely purposeless and playful. In this latter form, it is not necessary for laughter, a response to a humorous occurrence, to lead to action.

Another form of personal incongruity that is often humorous is a moral defect. A frequent object of humor and someone considered morally deficient is an avaricious individual, which is especially true in Indian culture that stressed generosity from very ancient times. The impact of this form of humor is borne very often by a member of the Brahmin caste, which appeals to caste stereotypes and prejudice, much like western ethnic jokes. After setting up his victim by telling him what a shrewd and calculating nature he possesses, Rāmakrishna replies that he is like a high caste priest who buys a cow that eats meagerly, gives plenty of manure, and produces a bountiful supply of milk.[25] A wealthy, clever, and deceitful man is exposed by Rāmakrishna's biting humor when the Master said, "'It isn't good to be clever. The crow is very clever, but it eats others' filth.'"[26] Even though Rāmakrishna was born a member of the Brahmin caste, he could still appeal to common cultural prejudice concerning the moral shortcomings of Brahmins: "'If a man doesn't give them money, they will call him bad; on the other hand, if a man is generous to them, they will call him good.'"[27] Rāmakrishna was not averse to indicating the humorous hypocrisy of allegedly pious individuals and common religious practices completed by someone without ethical integrity. If a religious person without strong ethical convictions bathes in the Ganges, all his sins are absolved because of the purifying powers of the holy waters. But what good is this act? Rāmakrishna indicates that popular belief teaches that sins lurk on the branches of the trees along the bank of the Ganges River. Just as soon as a person returns from the sacred river after bathing in its purifying waters, the old sins leap upon one's body from their concealment in the trees.[28]

Not only do people find physical deformity, ignorance and moral deficiencies funny, they also perceive human actions that fail as humorous. Informed by a follower that the autumn chill was conducive to good health, Rāmakrishna was returning home in a carriage and decided to try out his free medical advice by sticking his head out of the window of the carriage. Rāmakrishna reported that he then became ill.[29] Another example concerns a student at M's school, who was beaten by his parents for visiting Rāmakrishna. With an affectionate smile, Rāmakrishna told him, "'You had better get a leather jacket; then the beating

[24]Ibid., p. 294.
[25]Ibid., p. 264.
[26]Ibid., p. 602.
[27]Ibid., p. 727.
[28]Ibid., p. 190.
[29]Ibid., p. 568.

won't hurt.'"[30] This anecdote implies that the humorous magnet of the local young people was understood in some circles as a corrupter of youth. The wide variety of Rāmakrishna's humorous repertoire is evident in the following example of actions that failed: Once upon a time, a Muslim saint went to visit the powerful and wealthy Emperor Akbar in order to ask for money. The saint overheard the Emperor praying to Allah for wealth. When the saint started to leave, the Emperor asked him to stay. After the Emperor finished his prayers, he asked the saint what motivated him to visit the Emperor. The saint replied, "You yourself were begging for money and wealth; so I thought that if I must beg, I would beg of God and not of a begger."[31]

Besides the incongruity that one finds in some object or person, certain situations can also be incongruous. Rāmakrishna, for instance, made fun of Vijay, a follower and ardent practitioner of *sankīrtana* when he said, "'. . . I am seized with fear when he dances; for the whole roof may crash!'"[32] Sometimes an incongruous situation can be combined with stupidity to produce a humorous tale:

> Once a jackal saw a bullock and would not give up his company. The bullock roamed about and the jackal followed him. The jackal thought: 'There hang the bullock's testicles. Some time or other they will drop to the ground and I shall eat them.' When the bullock slept on the ground, the jackal lay down too, and when the bullock moved about, the jackal followed him. Many days passed in this way, but the bullock's testicles still clung to his body. The jackal went away disappointed.[33]

This anatomical type of odd situation combined with lack of knowledge can overlap with normal biological needs. Rāmakrishna relates that a child asked its mother to wake it in order to heed the call of nature when going to bed for the evening. The mother replied to the child that it was not necessary to worry because the call of nature will awaken you.[34]

Like the silent screen comedian Harold Lloyd hanging precariously over a street from a tall building, life and death situations can be funny. Rāmakrishna told a story about a man who had acquired the power to tame ghosts. When a ghost responded to his summons it was given work to do. The ghost, however, threatened the man that if it did not have any work to do it would break the man's neck. At first, the man had no trouble finding work for the ghost to complete. At last the man could no longer find any work for the ghost, who reminded the man of their original compact. The man asked for a moment's respite, and rushed to his teacher to find a solution to his dilemma. The man's wise and cleaver teacher instructed him to tell the ghost to straighten its kinky hair, an impossible task to which the ghost now devoted all his time and energy

---

[30]Ibid., p. 606.
[31]Ibid., p. 656.
[32]Saradananda, II:803-04.
[33]M, p. 349.
[34]Ibid., p. 469.

without a chance of success.[35] Wonderful stories like this one help us to see human beings at their most vulnerable, as they are stretched over an abyss of darkness or an impossible situation, but not without hope of eventual triumph. Rāmakrishna's comic perception of the absurdity of certain situations potentially opens up the possibility for deeper insights into the human condition.

The second major type of humor is the mistaken perception of one thing seeming to be another of which a common motif is the humor of mimicry. Much like a clown wearing a top-hat, carrying a useless cane and attaché case in order to lampoon the wealthy businessman, Rāmakrishna reportedly imitated a wealthy, lavishly dressed, haughty woman doing *sankīrtana*. In order to draw attention to herself the wealthy singer would cough and then humorously blow her nose, raising her nose-ring.[36] The young devotees surrounding Rāmakrishna found, according to M, the Master's impression very convincing and funny. On another occasion the Master imitated a drunk with red eyes, a staggering walk, and confused speech before his wife.[37] Rāmakrishna was also a successful impostor of Hanumān, the monkey hero and assistant of the hero Rāma, Rādhā, the consort of Krishna, a Muslim and Christian.

Coincidence is a third type of incongruity, which includes the unexpected repetition of events or words. Rāmakrishna said that the cow suffers agony because it sonorously utters "I! I!" continously. It is killed by a butcher who turns the cow's hide over to another craftsman who makes shoes; its hide can also be made into a drum that is beat without mercy marking no end of its suffering.[38] The calf and pronoun are not funny by themselves, but when they are juxtaposed an incongruous event is created that is humorous. The repetition and confusion of words can also be funny. Rāmakrishna told a humorous tale about a barber who cut a man while shaving him. The man vehemently exclaimed, "Damn!" Because the barber did not know the meaning of the sudden utterance, he refused to finish shaving the man until the patron told him the meaning of the term "damn." The patron asked the barber to continue shaving him but to be more careful with the razor, insisting that the word did not mean anything. The barber was persistent in his refusal to continue to shave the man and his desire to know the meaning of the strange term. The barber replied that if "damn" possesses a positive meaning, then he and all his family, past and present, are "damns." If the term means something negative, then the patron, all his family, and ancestors are "damns."[39] The repetition of the same key term combined with ignorance makes this story amusing in any language. Rāmakrishna's humorous stories call his followers to use their imaginations; it renders forth a call to devoted followers to let their creative faculties overflow.

The juxtaposition of opposites is the final type of humor. Rāmakrishna said, "'The devotee of God wants to eat sugar, not to become sugar.'"[40] Again,

---

[35]Ibid., p. 790.
[36]Ibid., p. 717.
[37]Ibid., p. 106.
[38]Ibid., pp. 633, 105.
[39]Ibid., pp. 667-68.
[40]Ibid., p. 133.

"'What a devotee Shivanath is! He is soaked in the love of God, like a cheese-cake in syrup.'"[41] The juxtaposition of the opposites—eating something and becoming it, love and cheese-cake—creates the incongruity. A religious message can be made by means of a creative juxtaposition by Rāmakrishna, who was convinced that the Goddess dwells in all beings including a tiger, but one would not embrace a tiger because the Goddess dwells within it.[42] Included within this type of humor would be violations of physical laws. Rāmakrishna said, for example, in essence that the mere taking of monastic vows are useless if one remains attached to the world. This kind of action is akin to consuming one's own spittle after it has been on the ground.[43] The incongruity can also be created by the violation of logical principles or a logical impossibility. For instance, Rāmakrishna said, "'The almanac forecasts the rainfall of the year. But not a drop of water will you get by squeezing the almanac.'"[44] Or consider the following remark by the Master: "'My uncle's cow-shed is full of horses.'"[45] The comedian is free to break the rules of logic or the rules governing the use of language because logic and language are his/her playthings. Furthermore, given the fact that many people acknowledged Rāmakrishna as an incarnation—a juxtaposition of human and divine—is also ludicrous, taking into consideration natural laws and principles of logic. In early Christian art Jesus is depicted as a crucified human figure with the head of an ass.[46] This artistic expression illustrates the comic absurdity of the early Christian position: the claim that God became man in historical time and place. In essential agreement with the spirit of the early Christian artist's depiction of Jesus with the head of an ass, Soren Kierkegaard, the nineteenth-century Danish religious thinker, called the cross-event the absolute paradox.[47]

By demonstrating his sense of humor to those whom he encounters, Rāmakrishna lets them know that he does not have rigid expectations of them and does not plan to be unduly demanding. Rāmakrishna's humor allows others to be comfortable in his presence without having to scrutinize their language and behavior for its impact on the Master. A follower need not worry about conforming to exacting standards of spirituality or discipline. The message of Rāmakrishna's humor is not simply to be yourself, but to not forget to examine yourself, although it is permissible to have fun while engaged in the process of self-examination.

COMIC FIGURES

---

[41]Ibid., p. 158.
[42]Ibid., p. 84.
[43]Ibid., p. 224.
[44]Ibid., pp. 476, 729.
[45]Ibid., p. 780.
[46]Cox, p. 140.
[47]S. Kierkegaard, *Philosophical Fragments*, trans. David F. Swenson (Princeton: Princeton University Press, 1962).

Before attempting to discern what the humor of Rāmakrishna means, although I have already given hints, one might first ask: What type of comic figure does Rāmakrishna resemble? Does Rāmakrishna play the role of the fool, clown, trickster or comedian? It can be demonstrated that Rāmakrishna shares common features with each of these comic figures, although important differences are also evident.

The figure of the fool, a mocker of the religious and political realms, shares some features with Rāmakrishna because they both confound human reason, profane the sacred categories, refuse to accept human pretensions with absolute seriousness, turn sense into nonsense, and transform order into disorder. A long tradition of holy fools exists in the Greek Orthodox Church and Roman Catholic traditions grounded in the words of Paul concerning the foolishness of the Christian message (I Cor. 1:18-31) and the injunction to be fools for Christ's sake (I Cor. 4:10). Inspired by Paul's words, the Christian fool made himself physically appear and behave ridiculous, forms of self-effacement, becoming thereby an object of mockery by people threatened by his antics.[48] A crucial difference between the fool and Rāmakrishna is that the former is in control, whereas Rāmakrishna is often at the mercy of the Divine Mother.

Rāmakrishna's humorous anecdotes and behavior share some features with the clown, who manifests a self-contradictory nature, a contempt for status, representing an impostor, and taboo breaker and victim.[49] Since the clown does not fit into the patterns and structures of society because of his/her undignified, unreasonable and idiotic behavior, he/she manifests a self-contradictory nature, implying that he/she can be both crude and gentle, mean and magnanimous, clumsy and agile, and so forth. Feeding a cat sacred food, having strange visions, behaving weirdly towards a statue of the Goddess, and continually losing his cloth when in an ecstatic state are just a few examples of Rāmakrishna's strange behavior for a temple priest. Ikkyū, a fifteenth-century Japanese Zen master, gained enlightenment and composed poems critical of the lechery and beastly behavior of ordinary people, but he also patronized the brothels and wineshops of Kyoto.[50] Among Native American clowns, the same kind of self-contradictory nature is evident. An Apache clown, for instance, wears a mask of scraped rawhide, moccasins, and a gee-string on his white painted, mostly naked body.[51] The Sioux heyoka—someone who receives a vision of a Thunder Being—does everything in reverse of normal beings. He rides, for example, backwards on his

---

[48]Hyers, p. 48.

[49]See Wolfgang M. Zucker, "The Clown as the Lord of Disorder," *Theology Today*, 24/2 (October 1967), pp. 306-17.

[50]See Sanford.

[51]Morris Edward Opler, *An Apache Life-Way* (New York: Cooper Square Publishers, Inc., 1965), p. 105. Although referring to jokes, Mary Douglas' point has relevance to the antics of Indian clowns: "It represents a temporary suspension of the social structure, or rather it makes a little disturbance in which the particular structuring of society becomes less relevant than another." in "The Social Control of Cognition: Some Factors in Joke Perception," *Man* 3 (1968), p. 372.

horse, wears his boots on the wrong feet, often walks backwards, and wears heavy clothing in the summer and goes naked in the winter.[52]

The clown demonstrates a contempt for status. Rāmakrishna criticized continually the pretensions of the higher castes, wealthy individuals, the arrogance of the learned and false religious convictions. In comparison, Ikkyū demonstrated contempt for military status by publicly brandishing a long sword which appeared genuine but was made of wood.[53] And he chose to wear dung-spattered cow blankets, instead of appropriate clerical robes, an indication of his contempt for the corrupt Zen Buddhism of his time.[54] Among the Pueblo and Hopi Indians, clowns burlesque the Kachina dancers by dancing out of time and rhythm, and stumbling around and grimacing.[55] Pueblo clowns have been known to venerate a doll as a saint.[56] By lampooning those with high religious and social status, the clown breaks down the boundaries between sacred and profane, superior and inferior, powerful and impotent, divine and human. In order to demonstrate his/her contempt for the structure of social ranks and their symbols, the clown plays the role of an impostor. Rāmakrishna was a priestly impostor because he was really, in the hearts and minds of his devotees, an incarnation. Ikkyū impersonated a genuine religious leader because of his illicit love affair in his old age with a blind singer, which was something a Buddhist monk was forbidden to do by monastic regulations. Native American Indians impersonated human beings by, for instance, dressing like women and exposing a huge, false vulva in public or donning a large, artificial penis and faking public copulation with a female clown.[57]

The final characteristic of a clown is the willingness to break taboos and receive punishment for it. It is at this point that Rāmakrishna fails to share in the nature of the clown because he did not consistently break religious and social taboos. In fact, his attitude is very orthodox and traditional within the context of devotional Hinduism.

Although there is evidence in his biographies of Rāmakrishna playing tricks and being tricked himself, he seems to share fewer features with the figure of the trickster, such as Ananse of the Ashanti, Nanabozho of the Ojibwa Indians of

---

[52]John G. Neihart, *Black Elk Speaks* (New York: Washington Square Press, 1972), pp. 159-63.

[53]Sanford, p. 38.

[54]Ibid., p. 28.

[55]Mischa Titiev, *The Hopi Indians of Old Oraibi: Change and Continuity* (Ann Arbor: University of Michigan Press, 1972), p. 255.

[56]Elsie Clews Parsons and Ralph L. Beals, "The Sacred Clowns of the Pueblo and Mayo-Yaqui Indians," *American Anthropologist*, 36, 4 (October-December 1934), p. 491.

[57]Alexander Stephen, *Hopi Journal*, ed. Elsie Clews Parsons, Columbia University Contributions to Anthropology 25, vol. 1, p. 386; Charles Lange, *Cochiti* (Carbondale: Southern Illinois University Press, 1968), p. 304; N. Ross Crumrine, "Čapakoba, The Mayo Easter Ceremonial Impersonator: Explanations of Ritual Clowning," *Journal for the Scientific Study of Religion*, 8, 1 (Spring 1969), p. 6.

North America, Inktomi of the Sioux Indians, and the so-called "tricky one" of the Winnebago Indians.[58] The trickster is an ambiguous and paradoxical figure: fooler and fool; wily and stupid; subtle and gross. His place in the world is unclear and uncertain. It is sufficient if he survives from one adventure or misadventure to another.

Like the Winnebago trickster, Rāmakrishna, the divine incarnation, appears as human and non-human, illustrating the ability to assume any shape. The trickster and Rāmakrishna serve as mediators between the divine and human beings. And both figures live in a world of games; they create a playful game of life.[59]

Rāmakrishna is, however, unlike the trickster in several ways. Nanabozho of the Ojibwa Indians creates the world and institutes cultural elements in similar fashion to Ananse, who spreads cultural forces, and the trickster of the Winnebago gives culture to humans by bestowing language upon them. Whereas the trickster is known as a wanderer, Rāmakrishna stays within the area of Calcutta most of his life. The trickster is engaged in the struggle to survive. On the other hand, Rāmakrishna's struggle is to achieve salvation and to convey his message. Finally, the trickster, like Ananse and the Winnebago figure, is known as a lecherous being with an insatiable sexual appetite, which he uses his cunning to satisfy, while Rāmakrishna is the exact opposite in a moral sense of the lascivious and thieving trickster.

Even though Rāmakrishna shares some similarities with the fool, clown and trickster, there are too many significant differences between them to be able to refer to Rāmakrishna as undisputably representing one of these comic figures. If Rāmakrishna cannot be totally classified as a fool, clown or trickster, is there some type into which he does fit? Because of his keen sense of humor, ability to tell humorous anecdotes, strange antics, spontaneous laughter and status as an incarnation in the minds of many followers, Rāmakrishna can be called a divine comedian. Rooted and moving within the world, the comedian affirms the sacredness and worth of life.[60] To liberate humans, to conquer dualities, to unite human beings with each other and a higher reality, to perceive the incongruities of life are goals that the divine comedian tries to help others achieve. Yet the divine comedian transcends the imperfect world, even though he is based in the world and within the absurdities of the human condition. In the *Bhāgavad Gītā*, Krishna states that he comes from age to age to restore righteousness (4.7-8), a

---

[58]See Robert D. Pelton, *The Trickster in West Africa: A Study of Mythic Irony and Sacred Delight* (Berkeley: University of California Press, 1980); Christopher Vecsey, *Traditional Ojibwa Religion and Its Historical Changes* (Philadelphia: The American Philosophical Society, 1983), pp. 84-100; Paul Radin, *The Trickster: A Study in American Indian Mythology* (New York: Philosophical Library, 1956): Mac Linscott Ricketts, "The North American Indian Trickster," *History of Religions*, Vol. 5, No. 4 (1966), pp. 327-50.

[59]Hyers, p. 173.

[60]See Nathan A. Scott, Jr., *The Broken Center: Studies in the Theological Horizon of Modern Literature* (New Haven: Yale University Press, 1966); Hyers, p. 97.

doctrine that implies that he has come before and will come again. Just as there is no final end to the coming of the incarnation, the divine comedian returns without end.

HUMOR, DISTANCE AND COHESIVENESS

Humor is paradoxical in the sense that it creates distance, yet it is also a cohesive force. On the one hand, humor gives one an opportunity to step back and take an insightful look at life. Humor, on the other hand, is something relational; it is something one shares and enjoys with other people. Unless one is insane and laughs alone at only what one perceives to be funny, even if it is not humorous, a normal individual laughs with others. With the exception of laughing in trance states, Rāmakrishna's humor is shared with his followers.

To perceive the incongruity in a situation allows one to disengage oneself from it and to gain a distance from it, which tends to give one a better perspective on things, persons and events. To gain distance from a situation enables one to free oneself from being dominated by a given situation and our emotional reaction to it.[61] Since humor can help one to achieve distance, it can also enable us to enter into dialogue with others because gaining distance is a propaedeutic step before beginning a dialogue. In this sense, the distance engendered by humor frees one to enter into a meaningful relationship with others. This is certainly true for Rāmakrishna and the gradual increase of followers around him.

If humor allows one to gain distance from the world, it also enables one to recognize that there is nothing important within the world in any absolute way. For a saint, like Rāmakrishna, humor can act as a form of detachment from the world and its many allurements. If nothing within the world possesses absolute significance, then, there is nothing that can monopolize one's attention and energy. This scenario simply enhances one's freedom from the world.

Although humor enables one to gain distance from the world and other beings, it also paradoxically possesses a uniting force. For instance, American television comedy programs are often not recorded before a live audience. When comedy program directors follow this procedure they will dub-in the sound of people laughing. Why follow this procedure? Television directors of comedy programs know that laughter is contagious, like some viral flu. When someone is laughing I am also liable to join that person in mirth, even if I do not know what is funny, which can often be the case with American television comedy. My laughter may reinforce my companion's laughter and vice versa. Not only do two laughing individuals have an effect on the intensity of each other's laughter, our laughter is something that we share together, which tends to unite us in a mutual, filial bond of companionship. Thus humor possesses an innate cohesive effect with its ability to unite individuals; of course, it can also have the opposite result. To joke, to make merry, to banter with others, or to enjoy mirth is to set aside for a moment one's worries, everyday cares and anxieties. It means to

[61] Morreall, pp. 104-06.

set aside the practical and mundane and indulge ourselves in the impractical and frivolous.

Because humor possesses a socially cohesive quality, it can be used to break the ice in uncomfortable social situations. An accomplished public speaker commonly begins an address with a humorous anecdote, and the speaker may sprinkle humorous stories or sayings throughout his/her address. This practice not only keeps the attention of his/her audience, it also allows the speaker, who is often a stranger to members of the audience, to in essence say that he/she is not a stranger but one in common with those listening to the lecture. To enable a stranger to become in a sense a member of the group is both the cohesive power of humor at work and its ability to transform someone from one thing to another. All humans have the potential of being transformed into mirth-makers, which is what Rāmakrishna attempted to accomplish with his followers from one perspective. To be so transformed implies that humans can welcome strangers and be welcomed in return, just as Rāmakrishna did with his followers and the way that they reciprocated by accepting him.

To accept and be accepted, to unite and be united, to transform and be transformed, to love and be loved, to be free and to make others free is the way of humor. It can be a path of innocence, but not without mature insight into the nature of things. And Rāmakrishna certainly possessed a childlike nature throughout his life. Overall, it is, however, a playful path, which frees one from the humdrum of the mundane world and allows one to see a glimmer of light in a sea of spiritual darkness.

HUMOR, FAITH AND PLAY

As noted above, humor can be cruel, malicious and even vulgar, and it can lead one toward arrogance, pride and a lack of empathy. These possibilities represent the various dangers of humor. Thus humor needs faith to avoid becoming, in addition to the dangers already cited, superficial, empty and helpless.[62] If this becomes the case, humor, without a grounding in faith, leads to despair. On the other hand, faith without humor leads to dogmatism and a lack of creativity and spontaneity.[63] Rāmakrishna is able to avoid these dangers because his humor is grounded in his faith in a greater power, Kālī. He illustrates the relationship between faith and humor in the following anecdote: A man reported to a friend that he had witnessed a house collapse with a terrific crash. His well educated friend did not believe him and tried to confirm the collapse of the house by perusing a newspaper. Since the friend could not find any news about such a disaster in the newspaper, he did not believe the first man's account of events, concluding that it must be false.[64] Rāmakrishna is saying that humor grounded in faith gives one the courage to take a chance.

---

[62]M. Conrad Hyers, "The Comic Profanation of the Sacred," in *Holy Laughter: Essays on Religion in the Comic Perspective*, ed. M. Conrad Hyers (New York: Seabury Press, 1969), p. 27.

[63]Ibid., p. 24.

[64]M, p. 864.

Faith based on humor gives us certainty and possesses a terrific power. Although the hero Rāma built a bridge across the sea to Sri Lanka, Hanumān, trusting in Rāma's divine name, jumped across the sea and reached the other side, which demonstrates the power of his faith. Another man wanted to cross the sea, and he had a friend write Rāma's name on a leaf and tied it in a corner of the man's clothing. Without knowing the nature of the charm, the man was instructed to simply walk on the water, but he was warned that he would drown if he lost faith. While walking on the water, the man suddenly had an intense desire to see what was tied in his clothing. Once he discovered that it was merely a leaf with the name of Rāma written on it, doubt entered his mind, and he sank under the water.[65] This story illustrates the close relationship between faith and humor and the need to dispel all doubts, if one is to gain the safety of certainty.

If faith and humor need each other to be authentic, what is the relationship between humor and play? More precisely, what do they share in common? Humor is a form of play. Hyers notes, "All humor is play, but all play moves within the polarities of seriousness and frivolity, of sense and nonsense."[66] Humor can be either non-serious or serious, whereas play transcends this dichotomy. Political humor might be considered by some people to be a non-serious type of humor. Yet, there is a sense in which humor and play share certain serious and non-serious features: they are both frivolous and without purpose, whereas their seriousness relates to the doing, being absorbed or lost in play or laughter, the response to humor. Play is not something serious for the player, and humor is not serious for the humorist, which is why one engages in these activities. Play and humor have no goal or purpose that brings them to some final conclusion, which is indicative of their nature to constantly renew themselves. Play and humor hold the player and humorist within their spell by drawing them repeatedly back into the game. Rāmakrishna illustrates this playful game by stating that the world is real as long as the Goddess makes us aware of our ego, which causes objects of perception to exist. Human beings are like vegetables on a fire jumping around in a pot calling attention to themselves. If the body is represented by the pot, if the mind and intellect are equivalent to the boiling water, if sense objects are the various vegetables, and if the ego is what calls attention to itself while jumping about, the fire is being, consciousness, and bliss (*sat, cit, ānda* or Brahman.)[67]

Play and humor also share an irrational quality, which is probably in part their attraction for Rāmakrishna, who continually claimed that he had no use for reason or learning.[68] This attitude is illustrated by the story of an ant who returned from a sugar hill with one grain of sugar, which filled his stomach, and another grain in his mouth. While returning to its home, it pledged to itself that

---

[65]Ibid., p. 87.

[66]M. Conrad Hyers, "The Dialectic of the Sacred and the Comic," in *Holy Laughter: Essays on Religion in the Comic Perspective*, ed. M. Conrad Hyers (New York: Seabury Press, 1969), p. 213.

[67]M, p. 243.

[68]Ibid., pp. 272, 104, 183, 255.

next time it would bring home the entire hill.[69] Since humor and play are something one enters into freely, they share the characteristic of being a voluntary activity. Finally, humor participates in the essence of play, its fun-element; in other words, it is fun to laugh and play.

The playfulness of Rāmakrishna's humor allows him to combine within himself three levels of humor: laughter of paradise; laughter of paradise lost; and laughter of paradise regained.[70] Since Rāmakrishna's child-like qualities are manifested by his behavior and acknowledged by others, the laughter of paradise is like that of playful, innocent, little children playing for the sake of playing, a sheer waste of time and energy. Rāmakrishna's humor can be interpreted as a return to an innocent, unitive, playful, and idyllic setting. His humor can also be understood to deal with absurdity, failure, evil, anxiety, and suffering— a paradise lost. It approaches these features of human existence playfully, which implies that Rāmakrishna's humor refuses to surrender, be controlled or destroyed by them because his humor refuses to acknowledge these dark aspects of life with absolute seriousness. Finally, since Rāmakrishna's humor is grounded in faith of the Goddess, it enables him to manifest the laughter of paradise regained, a laughter beyond good and evil. Rather than the tensions and conflicts characteristic of faithless and unenlightened existence, Rāmakrishna's humor manifests inner harmony, resolution and unity. The laughter of the past, present and future paradises are united in Rāmakrishna, who is free to spontaneously dance, sing, laugh, creatively imagine all kinds of wonders and play.

Although humor is grounded in seriousness, as stated above, to be too serious indicates one's state of attachment and subsequent bondage, a grasping unto what is safe. Rāmakrishna intends to say that it is permissible to be serious about the right things, like one's spiritual development. But do not be too serious, do not be overly earnest, do not become imprisoned by one's sincerity and do not become attached to the outcome of one's actions to help others or oneself. Allow oneself a chance to enjoy a good laugh or tell a joke. By following this path, one can transform the world from a state of bondage into a realm of mirth, which does not have to be an extraordinary place. In fact, it can be very ordinary and very funny as the following story of Rāmakrishna illustrates about a young man proudly walking along a road showing off his fancy shirt. Trying hard to get people to notice his fine shirt and vainly looking about to see how many people were noticing him and his shirt, people could see that he was knock-kneed as he strutted down the road.[71] This young man is analogous to a peacock that displays its fine feathers, although it humorously possesses dirty feet.

Rāmakrishna's humor is indicative of his state of liberation. Since he did not manifest despair when he contracted cancer, and since he continued to laugh and make others merry, he was not in a state of bondage. His humor freed him from self-imposed delusions and gave him insight, which he attempted to share with others through his humor, into the depth of human delusions by calling

---

[69]Ibid., p. 577.

[70]See Hyers, *The Comic Vision*, pp. 33-37; I have adopted his insights for Rāmakrishna.

[71]M, p. 855.

into question the common sense understanding of the world. Those who could respond with laughter to the humor of Rāmakrishna and to perceive the incongruities of life were on the path to spiritual liberation. For Rāmakrishna, humor is both a prelude to enlightenment as well as a manifestation of it. If the ability to laugh places one on the path to enlightenment, the enlightenment experience itself often triggers laughter. If the ocean is a metaphor for the absolute, Rāmakrishna elucidates the relationship between humor and the unitive experience by telling the story of the salt doll that desired to measure the depth of the ocean because it wanted to be able to inform others of its depth. When the salt doll tried to measure the depth, it dissolved after entering the water.[72]

To be liberated, for Rāmakrishna, implies the ability to laugh at oneself, others and the foolishness of the world, an ability that places one beyond the binding power of the world and one's own self-delusions. Rāmakrishna makes fun of himself by telling the humorous story of a naked person, a world-renouncer who has attained the highest level of spirtitual perfection, who would emerge from his own body and walk with him as they talked and joked. Rāmakrishna relates that he saw other divine forms, which increased his pain from indigestion. Even though he would spit on the ground when he saw these visions, the visionary beings would persue him. He admits to being overwhelmed by his ecstatic visions to the extent of loosing track of time. After a profound vision at one time, he had an acute attack of diarrhea and tells us that "all these ecstasies would pass out through my bowels."[73] Since humor possesses the power to shift one's center of gravity from work, a confining and limiting position, to that of play, a status of freedom, it can awaken one to one's true humanity and spiritual center. Moreover, by affirming and not denying the incongruities of life, Rāmakrishna's humor gives one hope. This is not a false hope nor an overly optimistic form of hope; it is rather realistic.

Although there are certain social and existential consequences of humor, as I have indicated, humor is more akin to a gratuitous gift. And even though there are hints that Rāmakrishna might have had an altruistic motive for some of his humorous stories, the true spirit of his humor is given without ulterior motive. The basic message of Rāmakrishna's humor is simply to enjoy. It is solely enough to enjoy, to be amused, to laugh, to make merry and generally just be playful.

---

[72]Ibid., p. 103.
[73]Ibid., p. 813.

Chapter VI

THE STRANGER

In many ways Rāmakrishna is a product of Indian culture, and he cannot be adequately understood outside of the Indian religious context. Yet there is a sense in which he represented something unique, even though religious figures like him have appeared in India before and will probably appear in the future. In this chapter, I want to demonstrate in what sense Rāmakrishna represents a stranger, using in a modified form the insights of Alfred Schutz. But what are the useful insights of Schutz and what are the differences between his approach to the subject and that of this chapter?

In Schutz's essay on the phenomenon, he conceives of the stranger as an out-sider who does not share the basic assumptions of the group encountered. Since the stranger does not accept the cultural assumptions of the newly encountered group, he/she tends to call into question the basic assumptions of the group. And thus the stranger is more willing to test and question the authority of a given tradition because he/she was never part of the historical formation by which certain values were accepted by a social group. From the perspective of the group, the stranger is a newcomer without a history.[1] When approaching a group the odd questioning newcomer is transformed from a disinterested observer into a possible member of the group. For the stranger, the cultural pattern of a group is transformed from remoteness into proximity; "its vacant frames become occupied by vivid experiences; its anonymous contents turn into definite social situations; its ready-made typologies disintegrate."[2] Schutz is suggesting that it is one thing to hold detached beliefs about the cultural patterns of a group, but it is an altogether different thing to experience these patterns of belief. In his essay that is full of implications for a theory of hermeneutics as much as explicating the features of the stranger, Schutz thinks that any pre-understanding that one possesses of another group based on one's own inherited cultural patterns proves to be inadequate because "it has not been formed with the aim of provoking a response or a reaction from the members of a foreign group."[3]

Even though the stranger may be transformed when encountering a foreign group and even though the encountered cultural pattern is transformed, Schutz argues that the stranger, by being shaped by his/her own cultural patterns, lacks a guide for interaction with the new group and an experiential test for his/her ac-

[1] Alfred Schutz, *Collected Papers II: Studies in Social Theory*, ed. Arvid Brodersen, Phaenomenologica, Vol. 15 (The Hague: Martinus Nijhoff, 1964), p. 97.

[2] Ibid., p. 98.

[3] Ibid., p. 98.

tual encounter with a new group. Hence the stranger encounters new surroundings that appear very different from what he/she is accustomed to experience and this shocks him/her by upsetting his/her own habitual way of thinking. The stranger is no longer comfortably at the center of his/her world because he/she finds oneself in a strange cultural environment. The stranger is also shocked to learn that he/she lacks any social status as a member of the encountered group. The odd questioning newcomer discovers oneself outside of the new group, without bearings, and without a unity of schemes of interpretation or expression.[4] Although the cultural pattern of the encountered group does not provide the stranger with shelter, it does offer a field of adventure that becomes a topic of investigation and a problematic situation. This brief summary of Schutz's essay on the highlights of his conception of the stranger informs the approach of this chapter but not in an uncritical manner.

Our discussion of Rāmakrishna as a stranger excludes Schutz's notions about objectivity and doubtful loyalty, attitudes of the stranger to the group. This chapter is mainly concerned with the stranger as an odd questioning newcomer who inquires about the basic assumptions of a society and tests its system of beliefs because of a need to validate for oneself its belief system. The influence of Schutz's essay is also evident when we discuss the adaptation of the stranger to the group and vice versa. Because Schutz views the stranger as an outsider who approaches a group and its cultural patterns trying to be accepted or at least tolerated, the major difference between this approach and the discussion of this chapter is that we will try to demonstrate that a stranger can emerge from within the cultural group. In other words, the stranger does not have to come, as Schutz seems to suggest, from outside of the prevailing group. As this chapter will demonstrate using Rāmakrishna as our evidence in contrast to Schutz's position, it is possible for someone to be a stranger and to still share many of the basic assumptions of the prevailing culture. Although there is no reason for Schutz to do so, he does not discuss the stranger as an incarnation and this person's relationship to the concept of play. Thus it is fair to say that the subsequent discussion is informed by Schutz's essay but is not slavishly limited to it because of the nature of our focus upon Rāmakrishna and his unique character and pattern of behavior.

This chapter is motivated by an implied agenda in *The Gospel of Sri Rāmakrishna* compiled over a period of four years by M, who faithfully recorded the Master's teachings, songs of devotion, reminiscences, and behavior. What makes M's work, thought and insights valuable to the topic of this chapter are his struggle to comprehend the significance of the religious message and nature of his subject. In other words, M pondered some of the following questions: Who is this odd, little man? What does he represent? Is he someone demonically possessed? Or is he a divine incarnation? Regardless of how these questions are finally resolved, M and other followers allow us to view Rāmakrishna as a stranger.

Within the Hindu tradition, there were two distinctive terms that were used to refer to strangers: *mleccha* and *yavana*. The first term referred to an outsider or

---

[4] Ibid., p. 99.

foreigner. This person was outside the ritualistic, religious, social and linguistic milieu of the prevailing Aryan community. The *yavana*, a designation used to later supplement the term *mleccha*, refers to strangers in a more radical way by invoking images of a barbarian or someone totally alienated from the social and religious *dharma* of the orthodox community. The difference between these two terms is made clear by Halbfass:

> *Yavana* is a more descriptive concept which refers to specific groups of foreigners, recognizes their factual peculiarity among other such groups, and indicates a certain degree of curiosity and readiness to differentiate. *Mleccha*, on the other hand, implies a much stronger value judgment, a religious-tabooistic exclusion. It identifies the foreign, the other as violation of fundamental norms, as deficiency, deviation and lack of value.[5]

Although *yavanas* may have a legitimate place in India, *mlecchas* have no proper place and Hindus are warned not to have contact with them. Having clarified these terms and noting their significance, it cannot be stated that Rāmakrishna could be characterized by either term because he represents something common yet unique to Indian religiosity. Rāmakrishna, his parents, wife, friends and followers were all born into an already established Hindu culture with a well defined pattern of acceptable behavior, which can be called orthopraxis, transmitted from antiquity by ancestors, teachers and revered cultural authorities. Tradition bestowed on these cultural patterns an unquestionable authenticity and authority, which were to serve as an unquestioned and unchallenged guide for life. Hindu cultural patterns made life less troublesome by offering established and efficacious directions for the individual to attain his/her goals. In a behavioral sense, truth was self-evident and self-explanatory. Thus one need not struggle from one perspective for the truth, which was already given in the cultural patterns and preserved for newer generations by sages. This easy path to the truth merely demanded adaptation to what was already given. Of course, certain basic assumptions had to be accepted in order to make one's adaptation efficacious: (1) that life and the solutions to problems would continue to be the same as it had been; (2) that one could rely on traditional knowledge; (3) that one could manage one's affairs if one knew something about the general pattern of events one might encounter; (4) that cultural patterns and their fundamental presuppositions are accepted and practiced by other beings within the given culture.[6] In contrast, particular cultural patterns and basic assumptions are not shared by the stranger, a free thinker who calls everything into question.

The Indian tradition has allowed for considerable freedom of thought for individuals to question the already established cultural and philosophical notions, but not its behavioral patterns. Referring to the yogis, Jean Varenne relates that Hindu society as a whole views them with mistrust. It has an ill-formulated feel-

---

[5]Halbfass, p. 176.

[6]Schutz, p. 96.

ing that these renouncers are defying *dharma*.[7] In fact, renouncers are a potential danger to orthodox society because they are a possible source of pollution to the orthodox community. Despite the mistrust and potential danger of pollution from renouncers, Indian culture has witnessed many strangers throughout its history, and many of them have come to find a home in India (e.g. Mahāvīra, Buddha, Śaṁkara, the Āḷvārs, Caitanya, etc.). For instance, Tukārāma, the poet-saint of Mahārāshtra, wrote about having become a stranger to his native village, former friends and cultural heritage.[8] By finding a niche in Indian culture, these original strangers have reinvigorated India's culture and become her sons and daughters.

In order to demonstrate the pattern of the stranger within Hinduism, this chapter will examine a nineteenth-century son of India and subject of this book. Actually, Rāmakrishna appears to be on the surface an unlikely candidate to function as a cultural stranger. Since he grew to adolescence in a typical, rural Indian village, learned many stories of the traditional epic and Purāṇic literature, associated with wandering holy men and women near his village, and participated in theatrical, religious performances, he appears to have been culturally endowed to a large degree. Although Rāmakrishna represents a thoroughly nineteenth-century Hindu and is not a stranger to Indian culture in the sense of being a foreigner, he manifests sufficient characteristics that allow one to justifiably refer to him as a stranger. After spending eight years at the temple in Dakshineswar as a priest, Rāmakrishna, for example, returned to his childhood village. He reportedly felt "like a man who had returned home from a far off place and to whom every person and object of the village appeared to be new."[9] Only a stranger would react in this way. Swami Saradānanda explicitly acknowledged that Rāmakrishna was a stranger because "he does not belong to any particular country, community, nation or religion."[10] Actually, Rāmakrishna possessed something in common with ancient Israelites who were aliens and wanders on the earth, and he can be compared to Christians, who throughout the centuries understood themselves as pilgrims in a foreign world. Rāmakrishna also shared something in common with the modern Indian leader Jawaharlal Nehru, who felt a queer mixture of East and West after his education at Harrow and Cambridge University. Nehru confessed that he felt out of place everywhere and sensed a profound alienation between himself and the religion of the common folk of his native country.[11]

---

[7]Jean Varenne, *Yoga and the Hindu Tradition,* trans. Derek Coltman (Chicago and London: University of Chicago Press, 1976), p. 134.

[8]Fraser and Marathe, 376, 384, 414, 458, 1298.

[9]Saradananda, I:306.

[10]Ibid., II:639.

[11]Jawaharlal Nehru, *Toward Freedom: Autobiography* (Boston: Beacon Press, 1958), pp. 236-50.

THE ODD QUESTIONING NEWCOMER

In the *Bhagavad Gītā*, Arjuna, a warrior and third oldest of the five Pāṇḍava brothers, is confronted with an ethical and religious dilemma: Should he fight and possibly kill his relatives and former teachers, who have usurped the kingdom that rightfully belongs to his father, him and his brothers, or should he renounce violence and the world? Both paths are viable options sanctioned by his culture. But which path is the correct option in his situation? The confused, compassionate and despondent warrior turns to a dialogical encounter with Krishna, the fighter's trusted charioteer, for advice and wise counsel. Although those influenced by Gandhi's nonviolent philosophy might be surprised, Krishna, having become the warrior's teacher (2.7), asserts that Arjuna must fight for four basic reasons: (1) the self is immortal and is not destroyed when the body dies (2:12-25); (2) what is born must die and what dies must be born again (2:26-29); (3) it is the duty *(dharma)* of the warrior caste to fight (2:31-33); (4) Arjuna would lose face and be accused of cowardice if he did not fight (2:34-37). Because Arjuna is a bit dim-witted, he continues to be confused after Krishna's counsel. As the dialogue between the two comrades-in-arms continues, Arjuna, assuming that he knew the identity of his companion, comes to learn of his friend's true nature in the eleventh chapter of the text, which represents the great theophany and culmination of the dialogical encounter. Although Arjuna thought that he knew the identity of his charioteer, he is surprised and stunned to discover that his friend is really a stranger. As the text makes clear, Krishna is an incarnation, having come to earth to restore righteousness (4:7-8). Krishna's revelation of his nature to Arjuna, for which the latter must be given a celestial eye to perceive god's nature (11:5-8) due to the inadequacy of human vision to encompass the total splendor and mystery of god, calls into question Arjuna's assumptions about his companion.

A similar type of revelation occurs in the life of Rāmakrishna. His sudden ecstatic trance states, his visions, apparent madness, assumption of female roles and his bizarre antics mark Rāmakrishna as odd. He is different than other people and seems to be a bit foreign. He does not fit into acceptable social patterns. In contrast to other people, Rāmakrishna's behavior is unpredictable. Thus he confounds and astonishes those who are predictable when they encounter him.

For those who feel safe and secure in their cultural patterns, the stranger creates uneasiness because he/she questions the basic assumptions of society. Since the intrusion of the stranger tends to disrupt the cultural view of the in-group, the stranger is immediately perceived by the established group as an outsider and a threatening figure. The stranger threatens accepted social structures and proprieties, he/she may overturn moral and ethical values cherished by the in-group, or he/she may pay little heed to accepted ways of adjudicating or avoiding social disagreements. He/she may also threaten the familiar sacred structure and traditionally accepted religious routine. Rāmakrishna, for instance, feeds an image of Kālī with his own hands, gives food destined for the Goddess to a stray cat and generally acts bizarre in the temple. Although the in-group disapproves of the stranger's behavior, they are often fearful of directly confronting him with their complaints. Some worshipers at the Kālī temple, for instance, witnessed

Rāmakrishna's antics and complained to the officers of the temple. "But when they saw Sri Rāmakrishna's excited, formidable visage, as of one possessed by a power, his unhesitating behavior and his fearlessness and absentmindedness, they shrank with an indefinable fear from mentioning anything to him or from forbidding him to do what he was doing."[12]

Although the group generally accepts unquestionably the authority of its given culture, it does not have the same unchallengeable character for the stranger; he must test the system to discover its validity for himself. One finds exactly this questioning attitude in the life of Rāmakrishna, who examined personally for himself the truths of devotional Hinduism, Tantra, Vedānta, Buddhism, Islam and Christianity. Rather than simply accepting what others believed, Rāmakrishna validated these religious paths for himself. Thus Rāmakrishna examined, experienced, confirmed and eventually accepted what others merely assumed to be the case. Even though Rāmakrishna discovered that these diverse paths lead to the same goal, his discovery of the truth of Islam and Christianity did not really become an integral part of his personal biography in the sense that he shared the history of those faiths.

From one perspective, the history of Hindus became a part of his personal biography only after he was able to validate it for himself, which implies that he was able to participate in the Hindu tradition of the past only after his own religious rite of passage.[13] No longer a man without a history (an experientially validated past), Rāmakrishna was able to share in the joy of the religious enthusiasm of the present moment and to offer hope for future religious fulfillment. Thus the established cultural pattern of Hinduism, for Rāmakrishna, was not an unquestionable given or matter of course; it was a field of adventure to investigate, to question, to experiment with, to disentangle and finally to master. The newcomer's questioning attitude is not necessarily destructive of the existing cultural pattern. In Rāmakrishna's case, he functioned as a revitalizer. Thus the newcomer need not be a total alien to a given culture to approach it as a field of adventure.

ADAPTATION AND HOMECOMING

As we have already observed, Rāmakrishna as a stranger, engaged in an inquiry and testing of the religious truths of Hinduism and other religions. Leaving aside the other religions and concentrating on Hinduism, there was a twofold process of adaptation occurring. On the one hand, Rāmakrishna was adapting to the demands of the prevailing cultural pattern, and, on the other hand, others were adapting to him. Since Rāmakrishna represented something extraordinary, unfamiliar and unknown to common experience, others began a process of inquiry.

From the perspective of those within the predominant culture, the best evidence that we possess of this process is found in *The Gospel of Sri Rāmakrishna.* Within this work, the reader is given a glimpse into the mind of

---

[12]Saradananda, I:168.

[13]This point differs with Schutz's position, p. 97.

M, who struggled to make sense from his religious cultural position of the Master's actions and words. M speaking to the Master acknowledged, "'Likewise, it is not possible to recognize you.'"[14] After Rāmakrishna made a reference to the 'sun at dawn' and 'the tree unrecognizable by man,' M silently pondered the significance of these references. Did Rāmakrishna mean to refer to an incarnation of god? Was the Master himself such an incarnation? How can I be certain what he means or represents? M struggled with such questions over a period of time. Rāmakrishna's relationship to Kālī was also confusing to M. He wondered to himself whether or not the Goddess had incarnated herself as a male in order to inform humankind about the ways of the Goddess.[15]

M's inquiry was an attempt to define this stranger, to assign him a meaning from within the facts offered by M's culture. After Rāmakrishna hinted that he might be an incarnation, M tried to analyze the evidence by pondering the fact that Rāmakrishna claimed that it is only possible for an incarnation to return to the phenomenal realm after having reached the state of *nirvikalpa samādhi*, the highest state of spiritual attainment.[16] Since M had witnessed the Master suddenly enter into an ecstatic trance and return to normal consciousness, it occurred to him that maybe the Master was trying to instruct him about the relationship between actions and words. Pondering the stranger, M said to himself, "'There is much similarity between Chaitanya and the Master.'"[17] M's observation is a perfect illustration of using a known entity from his religious culture to interpret the strange fact that he has encountered. By transforming what is strange into something compatible within one's experience, the puzzle loses its problematic nature and becomes a part of one's own given body of knowledge.[18] When the strange entity fits into our pattern of knowledge it becomes not only an additional element of our epistemological repertoire, but it also ceases to be strange. Thus one's knowledge is expanded, one's expectations are altered and one's cultural patterns are broadened.

Since the process of adaptation involves a two way process, the stranger adapts to the in-group by inquiring into the cultural pattern of the in-group. "If this process of inquiry succeeds," writes Schultz, "then this pattern and its elements will become to the newcomer a matter of course, an unquestionable way of life, a shelter, and a protection."[19] This occurred to Rāmakrishna to a large extent because he became very comfortable with his devotees, enjoyed their shared devotions and even became anxious when someone did not visit him for a time, which was especially true of his concern for the whereabouts and welfare of Narendranāth (later Swami Vivekānanda). What is unique about Rāmakrishna's playing the role of a stranger and the process of adaptation is that others tended to adjust to him and not vice versa. Rāmakrishna's wild behavior is tolerated, his humor is appreciated, his love of sweets is indulged, his words are listened to,

---

[14]M, *The Gospel of Sri Rāmakrishna*, p. 283.
[15]Ibid., p. 301.
[16]Ibid., p. 358.
[17]Ibid., p. 330.
[18]Schutz, p. 105.
[19]Ibid., p. 105.

his company is eagerly sought, his child-like behavior is found amusing and charming, his housing is provided for him and his meals and bodily comforts are provided. Why was the process of adaptation so one-sided? After Rāmakrishna was recognized as an incarnation by his devoted followers, he was fitted into their cultural pattern. Since Rāmakrishna was believed to be an incarnation, he was due certain respect which was appropriately rendered by his followers.

In sharp contrast to the role of the stranger played by Rāmakrishna is Meursault of Albert Camus' novel *The Stranger*. Meursault represents a much different type of stranger than Rāmakrishna, because the former is an anonymous man with nothing to say to others or contribute to society. Meursault is a callous person with no moral qualities, imagination, or concept of truth. Absorbed in the present moment, he is unable to believe in anything or unable to love anyone. He can only follow his sexual urges, but he is incapable of establishing a meaningful, loving relationship with a woman. When Marie, his mistress, asked Meursault if he loved her and would he like to get married, he replied that her question lacked meaning and a decision to get married was of no real importance.

Meursault is indifferent and detached from common events of life. He is, for instance, indifferent to his mother's death for which he could not shed a tear or bear to view her remains. He complains that her death is not his fault, and he acknowledges that even with her death nothing in his life had changed to any significant degree. When his employer asked him if he would like a transfer to Paris and a change of life, Meursault replied indifferently that one never changed his way of life. In fact, one life was as good as another.

Life, for Meursault, is without meaning which implies that ethical decisions are of no consequence. His choice to kill or not to kill the Arab did not really matter because nothing mattered, and whatever his final ethical decision would be it would result in absolutely the same thing. In fact, it did not matter if he fired one or five shots into his victim's body. Moreover, he demonstrates no remorse for his violent action. But why is life meaningless for him?

For Meursault, there is no God to give life meaning, a position diametrically opposite to the religious convictions of Rāmakrishna. During an examination, the local magistrate, who was puzzled by the man and his crime, thrust a silver crucifix under Meursault's chin and asked him if he believed in God. The murderer gave a negative reply. The magistrate, a representative of the community in this story, is convinced that even the worst of sinners could obtain forgiveness if one repented of one's sins. It is unthinkable to the magistrate to doubt or deny the existence of God because without a divine being life would lose all meaning. In contrast, Meursault thought that it is absurd to feel like this. Since Meursault flouts without compunction the cherished assumptions of the community, there is absolutely no place for him within the social fabric.

STRANGER AS INCARNATION

Due to the fact that Rāmakrishna was born, raised, partly educated (he did not appear to have been successful in school and essentially lost interest in learning with the exception of religious knowledge) and lived his life within the Indian cultural milieu, one could argue that he was not a stranger to the prevailing cultural patterns of his time. And this argument would be partly true, but it does not encompass the whole of Rāmakrishna's life and teachings and what he represented to his followers. Thus such an argument, as the one above, would fail if one tried to incorporate the doctrine of incarnation and the concept of play. Why would a counter-argument to the case made in this chapter fail if one considered Rāmakrishna as an incarnation? An historical incarnation is by its very nature a stranger to whatever culture it encounters because a god-man is not something an ordinary person meets very frequently or at any time. The incarnation represents an oddity, an aberration, a coincidence of opposites, an absurdity and a miracle. Since the nature of an incarnation—human and divine—does not resemble those around him, he is a stranger to those that he encounters.

Like Jesus and Krishna, Rāmakrishna's home was not of this world. Since he was a stranger to this world, the incarnation was an itinerant pilgrim on foreign soil. If his real home was heaven or some transcendental state of being, the incarnation was like the stranger an alien on the surface of the earth.

Because the stranger-incarnation was an earthly alien, it was difficult for the in-group that he encountered to discern his true identity. The stranger-incarnation metaphorically wore a dark mask to hide his true nature. Rāmakrishna was sensitive to the problems of recognizing the stranger-incarnation. He admitted that when the Goddess incarntaes herself she behaves like an ordinary human being, and this makes it difficult for anyone to recognize an incarnation.[20] Ordinary mortals are left dumbfounded when they encounter the strange god-man. To Hindus and those of other religious persuasion, a genuine incarnation was not only something wonderful and rare, but it was also something so totally striking, bewildering, bizarre and beyond one's ken that the person who embodied the incarnation was seen as fundamentally different—as strange or as a stranger.

On the other hand, the stranger-incarnation possessed absolute certainty which was derived from his personal, intuitive knowledge. This type of knowledge, which was self-validating, gave the stranger a direct insight into truth, the good and the real.[21] Due to its self-validating and direct nature, this type of knowledge was invincible and lacking nothing in its completeness.

When the time was right on earth and when human circumstances warranted it, the divine incarnated itself on earth to alleviate human misery. By an act of his own free, playful nature, god or the goddess chose to be incarnated. Therefore, granting with Rāmakrishna's followers that he represented an incarnation, he was in a sense a stranger by his own free choice. But why did he make such a decision? M recorded a number of reasons given by Rāmakrishna: to bring spiritual knowledge to human beings;[22] to teach humans the ecstatic love of the deity;[23] to enable humans to hear his words; to play through his incarnational body.[24] Although Rāmakrishna recognized himself as a stranger-incarnation with

---

[20] M, p. 361. 168.
[21] Hartt, p. 127.
[22] M, pp. 272, 359.
[23] Ibid., p. 283.
[24] Ibid., p. 782.

a salvific purpose, it is unclear from his recorded words if he understood the scope of his mission to be intended for a small group, for all of India, or for the entire world.[25]

As noted previously, M struggled to make sense of the stranger that he encountered near Calcutta. Finally, M became convinced that Rāmakrishna was an incarnation, although M confessed that he was unsure of the extent of the divine manifestation.[26] In other words, M was not certain if Rāmakrishna represented a full or partial manifestation of the divine. Other followers also recognized Rāmakrishna as an incarnation as did Rāmakrishna himself. Since he and his followers were convinced that he was an incarnation, M recorded an unusual event: a flower-basket and sandal-paste were placed before Rāmakrishna as he sat on the bed. Rāmakrishna, the object of these devoted offerings, proceeded to worship himself with these items by placing the flowers and sandal-paste on various parts of his own body.[27]

This incident clearly demonstrates the stranger worshiping himself or offering adoration and obeisance to the divine nature within himself. This unusual episode suggests a homecoming for the stranger. It also represents an acceptance by Rāmakrishna of what he is, and a devotional acknowledgment of his true nature by his followers.

In contrast to the mutual or, at least, partial adaptation of Rāmakrishna and his followers, the stranger of Camus' novel is not able to adapt to the in-group because of his nihilistic convictions. During his trial, Meursault becomes aware that there is a communal conspiracy to exclude him from the legal proceedings. He comes to realize that he is a "sort of gate-crasher," a stranger. The community views his violent action, lack of regret, and beliefs as a threat to its own security. Even thought the jury renders a favorable verdict under the circumstances, the judge condemns him to death, an attempt to totally eradicate a social irritant and threat to the social fabric.

There is no homecoming for Meursault, a man without place, feelings or acceptable beliefs. Meursault, a stranger, can only await his death in his lonely prison cell, unrepentant and without empathy to the end, regardless of the sincere efforts of the prison chaplain to communicate with him. To his impending death, Meursault's reaction is his belief that life is not worth living. Since everyone must die sometime, his death is of little consequence because life will continue on as before when he is gone. For Camus' stranger, there is no hope because there is no meaning, a philosophical position that Rāmakrishna could never comprehend.

---

[25]Matchett thinks that Rāmakrishna did not perceive himself as a saviour of India or the world, p. 179.

[26]M, p. 715.

[27]Ibid., p. 959.

THE STRANGER AND PLAY

A primary reason for the incarnation of Rāmakrishna was simply play, a manifestation of the *citśakti*.[28] By means of her *śakti* (creative, feminine power), the Goddess incarnated herself as a man in order to sport on earth and to instruct human beings in the ecstatic love for her.[29] As the playful incarnation, Rāmakrishna assumed the role of a stranger, whose presence called into question one's fundamental assumptions and one's understanding of oneself. The stranger-incarnation thus motivated one to reexamine oneself and in the process to redefine and rediscover one's true identity. The stranger helped one to redefine what one was, what one should be and what one can be. Within this process of rediscovery, one was the plaything of the divine, who playfully helped one recognize one's current condition of bondage, that one should be loving, and that one can be liberated from suffering, ignorance and rebirth.

Because the stranger-incarnation disrupted the security of one's common assumptions and motivated a self-examination, which could prove to be an arduous and painful process for the individual, Rāmakrishna played the role of a spoiler. In other words, the arrival and influence of the stranger means that nothing will ever be the same again. The game of life and the rules of the game are now inexplicably altered to conform to the stranger's mode of play. If one wants to be a member of the stranger's team, one needed to adhere to his way of playing. To complain about the altered style of play was to be recognized as a spoiled-sport. The basic message was: join the stranger's team, play with all one's energy and have fun.

Rāmakrishna, the stranger-incarnation, also played the game of "Who am I?" In this mode of play the stranger confounded, amazed and dazzled the other players. Rāmakrishna claimed not to be a stranger, which tended to confuse others because they were convinced that he was a stranger. The Master, for instance, spoke directly to M in the company of other followers, and he related that he was not an outsider. Furthermore, he said that he saw *satchidānanda* (ultimate reality, Brahman) emerge from his body, which proceeded to announce that it incarnated itself in every age.[30] The devotees listened to these words in utter amazement, wondering whether god was actually seated before them in the form of Rāmakrishna. During an *āratī* (waving of lighted oil-lamps) ceremony at the temple attended by many women, an unknown woman began fanning the Goddess, radiating an unexpressible beauty from her person, dress and ornaments, according to Mathur Babu who could not determine her identity. Later he asked his wife about the identity of this strange woman. His wife confessed to his complete surprise that the mysterious person was Rāmakrishna fanning the Goddess in an ecstatic condition dressed as a woman.[31] Thus the divine player overwhelmed the mortal players, who were left in their perplexed conditions to wonder what next.

---

[28]Ibid., p. 290.

[29]Ibid., pp. 460, 283.

[30]Ibid., pp. 720, 144.

[31]Saradananda, I:513.

The stranger who falsely claimed not to be an outsider brought what was alien to those that he encountered. The alien element was divine play, which the stranger incorporated into his performance given on the stage of human existence. Since the Master was hungry, about two pounds of sweet pudding was prepared, for example, and brought to him by a female devotee. She was startled to see the master walking about in the dead of night with a body that had become much larger in both height and bulk. Since his appearance bore no resemblance to an earthly mortal, she concluded that someone else must be within him eating pudding to which the Master concurred with a smile.[32]

The element of divine play, a joyful, purposeless activity, was also infused into the community that the stranger-incarnation encountered during his performance. The mortal players were wrenched free from the security of their unconsciously accepted cultural patterns. Once they were free, there was a strong compulsion to join in the fun. There was, however, no absolute guarantee that they would win. Like any game, there are winners and losers, but this was not really significant. What was important was playing the game, taking a risk, giving it a try and being a good sport by playing according to rules established by the divine player. Actually, it made no difference even if the game lacked rules.

If the heavenly realm represented a divine playground, and if the stranger-incarnation embodied the divine-player, the stranger tried to create a divine realm on earth modelled on the divine playground, much like a Hindu temple that is patterned on the square space of heaven. M recorded numerous examples of Rāmakrishna dancing intoxicated with the love of the divine with his devotees dancing around him in an ecstatic frenzy of joy. Rāmakrishna gave his followers a fore-taste of heavenly bliss.

As the divine stranger lost his mysterious quality and became accepted by the in-group, he became a *tīrtha*, a place of pilgrimage for others.[33] Followers journeyed to visit him, and they brought others with them. Rāmakrishna's followers felt a need to be near a source of holiness because the Master possessed a nourishing and purifying power similar to sacred water. As a *tīrtha*, Rāmakrishna formed a link between the mundane world and the transcendent much like the incarnation who combined the divine and human in one nature. By uniting heaven and earth, Rāmakrishna represented a threshold or a bridge from which to launch one's spiritual journey. A path open to all regardless of caste or sex allowed one to transcend earthly limitations. Therefore, Rāmakrishna invited his devotees to take a twofold spiritual journey: an external journey to the stranger-incarnation and an internal passage or crossing within themselves. This twofold crossing was really a unitary journey with two movements, one physical and the other spiritual. One was invited to be an itinerant traveller, a seeker after the truth, and a stranger to the world.

In Camus' powerful novel, the stranger, while he waits in jail, finds a newspaper account of a murder in a village in Czechoslovakia within the mattress of his bed. Meursault is fascinated by the story of a mother and sister who

---

[32] Ibid., II:580-81.

[33] See Diana L. Eck, "India's Tīrthas: 'Crossings' in Sacred Geography," *History of Religions*, Vol. 20, No. 4 (May 1981): 323-44.

murder a close kin they fail to recognize for his money. Meursault's reaction to the murder story is curious; he thought that the man was asking for trouble because he should not have played such a fool trick on his mother and sister. Unlike Rāmakrishna, Meursault is unable to recognize the importance of play for an enjoyable life.

Chapter VII

VISIONS

A beautiful, pregnant woman emerged from the Ganges River, gave birth to a child and began to tenderly nurse it. The comely mother figure turned suddenly into a horrifying hag and seized the infant with her jaws, grinding and crushing the little victim between her terrifying, dangerous teeth. After swallowing the tasty morsel, she returned to the sacred waters and disappeared.[1] It is not difficult to imagine that Rāmakrishna was left speechless and astonished by this vision of the two aspects—creative and destructive—of Kālī's nature. If madness can be construed as an outward manifestation of Rāmakrishna's sainthood, his visions, then, can be comprehended as an inward sign of his holiness. His biographers frequently recount that Rāmakrishna would suddenly pass into a trance state; sometimes the Master gave accounts of the visions that he witnessed during these trance states. This chapter will attempt to make sense of these visions by trying to interpret them within a comparative context. Since visions played such a central role among the Plains Indians of North America, I will use their vision quest and the experiences of some Christian saints and mystics as comparative materials in order to place Rāmakrishna's visionary experiences within a wider religious context. By following this comparative procedure, we will be able to indicate similarities and differences, broaden our horizons and understanding of visions, and to open potentially interesting areas for future research.

Within a cross-cultural context, visions may include hallucinations, dreams, unusual auditory or visual stimuli, possession by a supernatural being and trance states. Thus one may receive a vision while awake or asleep; either situation is usually considered by the visionary to be equally valid. Numerous scholars often refer to these phenomena as ecstatic types of experience, but this type of experience appeared to occur infrequently to Rāmakrishna.

To have an ecstatic experience implies to be beside oneself or to go beyond oneself. Rāmakrishna informed M that he had an ecstatic experience of nondual consciousness, which revealed innumerable kinds of creatures to him of different types and status. These creatures, ranging from lower animals to humans of various types and including Rāmakrishna himself, were fed a few grains of rice in this vision by the indivisible consciousness. This vision formed the context for Rāmakrishna's ecstatic experience. He reported to M that he saw rice, vegetables, and other kinds of food, along with some filth and dirt lying on the ground. When suddenly his soul left his body to touch the various kinds of food and filth, imagining his soul to be like a tongue of fire that tasted every item pre-

[1] M, p. 870; see also Saradananda I.232.

sent. This sublime experience revealed to him that his soul and all the substances, even the excrement, are a single, non-dual reality.[2] Although this was a profound ecstatic experience for Rāmakrishna, this type of ecstatic vision was an exception in his life rather than a common feature. Furthermore, Rāmakrishna's experience in this instance is to be distinguished from a mere enthusiasm for the divine because his leaving of himself was connected with a fulfilling and certain power, nondual consciousness. Based on the reports of M, the vast majority of Rāmakrishna's experiences are not ecstatic, but rather grounded in *samādhi* (absorption) or enstasis, as Eliade calls it.[3] For example, while in a boat passing the Manikarnika Ghāt on the Ganges River, Rāmakrishna had a sudden vision of Śiva. The boatman feared that Rāmakrishna might fall into the river because he stood near the edge of the boat and entered *samādhi*. Śiva stood at a distance on the ghāt; then the ascetic deity approached Rāmakrishna and merged into him.[4] Thus ecstasy, a going out or transcending of oneself, is the exact opposite of *samādhi* because the latter involves a withdrawal back into one's being or an interiorization of one's experience.[5]

Since Rāmakrishna's behavior manifested madness, as reviewed in chapter four, it is necessary to indicate that his visions are not a manifestation of psychotic fantasy, a private set of incommunicable images. As Obeyesekere[6] makes lucid, fantasy is an inner turmoil of an afflicted person trying to represent his/her inner state in outer images, which merely communicates to the culture that one is sick and needs assistance. In other words, psychotic fantasy possesses no cultural meaning. In contrast, the visions of Rāmakrishna are not without cultural meaning because they are expressed in a commonly accepted religious idiom, which contains mythic models that make the visions of the individual intelligible to the public. Rather than using fantasy, Rāmakrishna conceptualizes his inner experiences, which are grounded in *samādhi*, in terms of accepted cultural symbols. Thus Rāmakrishna's visions represent a cultural idiom constructed of interconnected symbols known and acknowledged as valid by others.

MOTIVATIONS AND RESULTS OF VISIONS

To the amazement of his followers and others, many of Rāmakrishna's visions came to him suddenly and unexpectedly, features that allow one to categorize such visions as spontaneous. Not all of his visions, however, can be classified as spontaneous. By investigating his life before his visions became very frequent or an integral part of his life, one finds that Rāmakrishna actively and agonizingly sought visions of Kālī early in his career. At one point in his life,

---

[2]Ibid., p. 282.

[3]See Mircea Eliade, *Yoga: Immortality and Freedom*, trans. Willard R. Trask, Second Ed. (Princeton: Princeton University Press, 1969), pp. 76-84.

[4]M, p. 803.

[5]Varenne, p. 136.

[6]Gananath Obeyesekere, *Medusa's Hair: An Essay on Personal Symbols and Religious Experience* (Chicago and London: University of Chicago Press, 1981), pp. 102-03.

Rāmakrishna was on the brink of despair of ever seeing the divine Kālī. Despair combined with an inner restlessness, unbearable separation from his loved one and conviction that life was worthless drove Rāmakrishna to the point of terminating his life when he spied the sword of the Goddess in the temple. After he seized the instrument that would end his misery, Kālī suddenly revealed herself obliterating everything else from his sight and revealing an infinite, effulgent, wonderful ocean of consciousness. After a terrific noise arose, Rāmakrishna gasped for breath and collapsed unconscious on the temple floor engulfed in undiluted bliss of the presence of the Divine Mother, which was Rāmakrishna's first vision of Kālī.[7] Thus we can summarize the primary motivation of Rāmakrishna as an attempt to realize the truth or his oneness with ultimate reality in the form of the Goddess.

In contrast, the vision seekers among Native American Indians of the northern plains would seek visions for the same reason as Rāmakrishna, that is, to gain knowledge. The Native American Indians would also seek visions in order to receive help in times of disease—one's own or that of a relative—and death. To insure bravery and success in warfare, an Indian would go on a vision quest before engaging in war expeditions or seeking revenge in battle and to obtain a supernaturally potent design for a war shield. Indians might also seek a vision at the birth of a child in order to discover the infant's proper name. Or an Indian might simply go on a vision quest as an act of thanksgiving for his/her good fortune in life.[8] With the exception of the final motivation for seeking a vision, these primary forms of motivation share something in common; they all emerge during periods of stress. If the seeker's stress is eradicated by his/her vision, this would seem to indicate that vision quests are a therapeutic process. Even though Rāmakrishna can be termed mad in the sense defined in chapter four, not all vision seekers need to be classified as sick, as Anthony Wallace claims.[9]

If one is motivated to seek a vision during a period of psychological and/ or physical stress, what are the common results of visions? Among Native American Indians, there are three basic results: (1) acquiring of ritual privileges; (2) receiving advice; (3) acquiring power. Black Elk, for instance, told John G. Neihardt that he was given the powers of healing and the ability to foresee future events. Black Elk did not totally comprehend his vision all at once. In fact, he learned the meaning of his vision as he grew older.[10] Crazy Horse, the great Sioux chief, was believed to be invincible on horseback, according to Black Elk, and his great powers, prestige and status were due to his visions.[11]

---

[7]Nikhilananda, pp. 13-14.

[8]Joseph Epes Brown, *The Sacred Pipe: Black Elk's Account of the Seven Rites of the Oglala Sioux* (Baltimore: Penguin Books, 1979), p. 46; Kathleen Margaret Dugan, The Vision Quest of the Plains Indians: Its Spiritual Significance, Studies in American Religion, Vol. 13 (Lewiston/Queenston: Edwin Mellen Press, 1985), p. 16.

[9]Anthony F. C. Wallace, "Revitalization Movements," *American Anthropologist,* 58 (1956), p. 273.

[10]Neihardt, p. 41.

[11]Ibid., pp. 70-71.

In contrast, Rāmakrishna did not need a vision to acquire ritual privileges that he already possessed as a temple priest. He was also not interested in acquiring power. In fact, he rejected the acquisition of power. This may seem strange within the Hindu religious tradition of ascetics and mystics known for their supernatural powers *(siddhi)*. Patañjali, to cite just one example, enumerates several mental and physical powers in the *Yoga Sūtra*: knowledge of past and future; ability to comprehend the sounds of all beings; knowledge of one's previous lives; ability to read the mind of another; knowledge of the universe; acquisition of great bodily strength and ability to fly.[12] Why did Rāmakrishna reject the acquisition of such powers?

He was convinced that powers beget pride, hinder the eradication of *māyā* (illusion) and, most importantly, hinder one from realizing ultimate reality.[13] Rāmakrishna's conviction was confirmed for him in a vision. Rāmakrishna's nephew Hriday wanted him to ask Kālī for some occult powers. After relating his nephew's request to the Divine Mother, Rāmakrishna was given a vision of Kālī, who produced a middle-aged prostitute sitting with her back to the Master. He could see her large hips and black-bordered sari before she became covered with filth. Rāmakrishna interpreted this vision to mean that occult powers are as abominable, according to Kālī's vision, as the dirt of the prostitute.[14] Thus the message of his vision given by Kālī confirmed what Rāmakrishna already suspected.

Although American Indians sought some result of their visions, Rāmakrishna, in contrast, sought visions as an end in themselves, which will become clear when we discuss play. The only thing that he seemed to gain from his visions was an intimate relationship with his beloved Kālī . In other words, his visions of the Goddess ended his feelings of separation from her and relieved his mental anguish.

TWO PHASES OF VISIONS

Among the Native American Indians, visions had two phases: quest and action. The former phase referred to the methods used to acquire a vision, and the action phase was a process by which an individual's vision was legitimatized. When there was a conformity between an individual's visions and actions,one's deeds and social status were considered legitimate. Thus visions gave one the right to claim certain powers, status and privileges. In this sense visions provided a link between the belief system of a tribe and its social structure because

---

[12]James Haughton Woods, trans., *The Yoga-System of Patañjali*, Harvard Oriental Series Vol. 17 (Cambridge: Harvard University Press,1914; reprint Delhi: Motilal Banarsidass, 1966), 3.16-3.42.

[13]M, pp. 158, 285, 624.

[14]Ibid., 745.

rights, duties and responsibilities were depended upon one's visions, which also gave an individual the confidence to assume certain social positions.[15]

A successful quest phase followed a common pattern among Native American Indians: (1) preparation by purifying baths; (2) sacred smoking; (3) nightly vigil; (4) meditation; (5) vision of some kind of spirit. This common pattern can be reduced to isolation and self-mortification.[16] In order to avoid confusion and giving the false impression that all American Indian vision seekers were successful, it is important to acknowledge that only those deemed worthy received the great visions. In contrast, we can assume that Rāmakrishna was considered qualified by the Hindu deities that appeared to him in his visions.[17] In order to more fully comprehend the overall pattern of the quest phase, it would prove useful to investigate more fully the Oglala Sioux rite of crying for a vision.

A propaedeutic step involved obtaining a holy man to act as one's guide.[18] With a sacred pipe filled with tobacco, one went to one's guide, entering his tepee with the stem of the pipe pointing forward. Sitting before the holy man, the pipe was placed on the ground with its stem pointing towards oneself which indicated that one wanted to obtain knowledge. After making a request for guidance, the aspirant and chosen guide left the tepee and faced west in order for the holy man to announce, with raised right hand holding the stem of the pipe to the heavens, that the seeker planned to offer his body in a few days. Seated in a circular fashion upon the ground, the holy man offered the pipe to the six directions, lighted it and passed it to the vision seeker, who offered the pipe up with a prayer before it was smoked by all those present. After a day to seek a vision was decided upon, the aspirant walked to the tepee of the holy man on the designated day, crying and wearing only his buffalo robe, breech cloth and moccasins. The seeker placed his right hand on the guide and asked for mercy and then placed the pipe in front of the holy man and asked again for his help. After the holy man asked the seeker how long (usually one to four days) he wanted to lament, the aspirant was purified in the Inipi lodge,[19] which consisted of heating stones, subsequent sweating to purify oneself, and a final offering of the tallow sealed pipe to Wankantanka (the Great Spirit).

With these ritual preliminaries completed, the seeker then isolated himself by riding to a chosen mountain or high site while crying most pitifully. The site of the vision quest was consecrated by digging a hole at the center of the site in which kinnikinnik, a bitter tobacco product, was placed; a pole was erected in the hole with offering tied at the top, and additional poles were erected at the four

[15]Patricia Albers and Seymour Parker, "The Plains Vision Experience: A Study of Power and Privilege," *Southwestern Journal of Anthropology*, Vol. 27, No. 3 (Autumn 1971), pp. 206-07.

[16]Ruth Fulton Benedict, "The Vision in Plains Culture," *American Anthropologist*, Vol. 24, No. 1 (January-March 1922), p. 1.

[17]Brown, p. 44.

[18]I have relied for information about the vision quest among the Oglala Sioux on Brown, 44-66, Neihardt, and William K. Powers, *Oglala Religion* (Lincoln. University of Nebraska Press, 1977), pp. 91-93.

[19]For a full account of purification see Brown, pp. 31-43.

cardinal directions. After undressing, the seeker walked alone on the sacred spot, holding the sacred pipe in front of him while carrying his buffalo robe. During the day, the seeker prayed out loud or silently at the center pole facing west and lamenting at each of the other poles of the cardinal directions. While grasping the pipe with both hands, the seeker prayed and asked for pity as he walked the sacred path between the poles forming a cross. The seeker slept on a bed of sage grass at night with his head leaning against the center pole, a representation of Wankantanka and source of his vision.

Among Native American Indians, the seeker often received a vision in animal form, although these animal spirits could change shapes from animal to human. Spirits were not restricted, however, to animals and could even be some inanimate thing.[20] In other words, the vision could continually transform itself, although it might follow any series of transformations. Black Elk, for instance, told Neihardt that he saw initially two men coming from the clouds carrying long spears from the points of which jagged lightning flashed. Then he saw a bay horse which spoke to him and told him to behold a series of twelve black, white, sorrel and buckskin horses. After the horses changed into various kinds of animals, he saw a cloud change into a tepee in which he perceived six old men, representing the powers of the world.[21] This vision occurred while Black Elk lay ill. It did not matter very much, however, whether one received a vision in a dream state or during a condition of waking consciousness.[22] Both types of vision were equally valid. The spirit frequently gave his protégé some supernatural skill or a requested medicine. Black Elk, for instance, was given the power to heal others. Instructions on the use of the gift and any taboo regulation associated with it were also given by the spirit. The spirit imparted medicine songs to some seekers in order for them to summon the spirit in dire times. Or the spirit described the appearance and contents of a medicine bundle, a visible sign of the spirit's presence, to be obtained by the seeker to be used whenever there was a need for assistance and protection by the spirit on the part of the seeker. After the seeker received a vision and possible message, he/she returned to the Inipi lodge for a final purification bath.

What is most apparent about the Sioux rite of crying for a vision is its ritualistic pattern. Although Rāmakrishna practiced isolation and self-mortification at times, the ritualistic pattern is generally not associated with his acquiring of visions, which often came unexpectedly and when Rāmakrishna was in the presence of other people. Rāmakrishna's visions of Kālī and other deities of Hinduism were different than the encounters of American Indians and their spirits. We have noted that Indian spirits, acting as benefactors, gave certain powers to seekers. Due to his low opinion regarding the effaciousness of spiritual powers, Rāmakrishna never asked the Goddess for such powers, as we have already indi-

---

[20]J. R. Walker, "The Sun Dance and Other Ceremonies of the Oglala Division of the Teton Dakota," *Anthropology Papers of the American Museum*, 16 (1917), p. 68.

[21]Neihardt, pp. 19-21.

[22]Clark Wissler, *Field Notes on the Dakota Indians, Collected on Museum Expedition of 1902* (New York: Museum of Natural History, 1902), p. 129.

cated. Like the American Indians, Rāmakrishna asked the Goddess for protection in an indirect manner. Rāmakrishna simply wanted the presence of Kālī, whose being in the form of a protective mother gave Rāmakrishna a feeling of security and well-being. Furthermore, the visions of Native American Indians were like omens of future events which fulfilled the visionaries' wishes for future success. In contrast, the visions of Rāmakrishna are without purpose.

Although the American Indians of the northern plains received their visions as individuals, a given vision or series of them was not simply a personal matter because it belonged to the entire tribe.[23] In contrast, Rāmakrishna's visions were very personal and not the property of the culture, even though he did comprehend his visions in terms of common cultural symbols. Another significant difference between American Indian vision recipients and Rāmakrishna is that the Indians were expected to relate the contents of their visions to a holy man, who was called a Yuwipi among the Oglala Sioux. It was the Yuwipi's responsibility to interpret the meaning of an individual's vision.[24] On the other hand, Rāmakrishna's visions were interpreted by him and were self-validating. Furthermore, the visions of Rāmakrishna had no economic value as they did among the Blackfoots who could sell visions to tribal members lacking them.[25]

If American Indians utilized isolation and various forms of self-mortification, like self-torture, fasting and thirst, to induce visions, what caused Rāmakrishna's visions? It has already been noted that Rāmakrishna practiced various forms of asceticism. What is unique about the origin of his visions in contrast to the American Indians is their often innocent or ordinary trigger mechanism. There are instances of Rāmakrishna going into a trance while singing,[26] at the sight of a picture of Jesus,[27] when he saw a prostitute dressed in blue and had a vision of Sītā,[28] the wife of the hero Rāma, and at the zoological garden when he spied a lion, the vehicle of the Goddess,[29] and was awakened consciously to Kālī. This is not to affirm that American Indians did not have sudden visions triggered by an ordinary experience. It is rather to assert that sudden visions were a much more frequent occurrence with Rāmakrishna and do not necessarily have to be associated with isolation or self-mortification. It is interesting to note that Rāmakrishna's disciples could often tell when he was gradually regaining normal consciousness because he would ask for a drink of water.[30] This demonstrates that his disciples became attuned to his conscious moods.

Another significant difference between the visions of Black Elk, for instance, and Rāmakrishna is that the former reported to Neihardt that he saw his original vision again later in life. Although Rāmakrishna reported that he also

---

[23]Dugan, pp. 17, 140.

[24]*William K. Powers, Yuwipi, Vision and Experience in Oglala Ritual* (Lincoln: University of Nebraska Press, 1982), p. 34.

[25]Benedict, p. 17.

[26]M, p. 107.

[27]Ibid., p. 826.

[28]Ibid., p. 231.

[29]Ibid., p. 391.

[30]Ibid., p. 465.

had similar visions again, he does make an interesting observation when he claims that the closer one moves spiritually to the Goddess the less one sees of her glory. He reported to M that as one initially progresses towards the Goddess one perceives her with ten arms, a more powerful manifestation of the divine; then, one may see an image with just two arms, devoid of the many weapons and gestures made by the many-armed figure. Next, one might have a vision of the tender child-god—Krishna—without any display of power. Beyond this type of vision, there are more abstract kinds of visionary experiences in which one sees only light.[31]

Rāmakrishna's instructive words assert that as one advances spiritually one sees less gross and physical types of visions of the divine. Embodied in his position is his conviction that reality transcends the most imaginative human conception of divine being, even though one can still maintain a personal encounter with reality. Thus Rāmakrishna combines *jñāna* (knowledge) and *bhakti* (devotion), which both arrive ultimately at the same goal or a state of *vijñāna*, something beyond union or identity with ultimate reality, something mysterious and beyond description.[32]

FUNCTIONS OF VISIONS

If we combine the evidence associated with Native American Indians and Rāmakrishna, we find that visions, a form of communication with the supernatural, manifests existential, psychological and social functions. These three functions tend to overlap with each other. Thus they will be differentiated in order to facilitate explanation.

We have already noted that tribal members receive powers and advice from the spirits in their visions. Although Rāmakrishna did not seek to gain powers from his visions, he did gain various forms of advice, messages or cures. The vision that Rāmakrishna had of Kālī giving birth and swallowing her infant revealed to him that everything is void.[33] Another vision cured him of a burning sensation in his body.[34] Late in his life, it was revealed to Rāmakrishna that during the final days of his life he would have to consume pudding. While his wife fed him pudding one day, he recalled his vision and burst into tears.[35] This episode gives us a glimpse of the human side of Rāmakrishna and his regret that death was so near and that he would soon be separated from those he loved.

It has already been noted that a vision quest motivates one's behavior and channels one's actions, legitimatizing some forms of action and not others. We have also seen that at times Rāmakrishna assumed a feminine mood and behaved like a woman. He asked Kālī for the ability to behave like Sītā, for instance, in a visionary experience.[36] A vision can also function to solidify one's identity to

---

[31]Ibid., p. 177.
[32]Matchett, p. 174.
[33]M, p. 870.
[34]Nikhilananda, p. 16.
[35]M, pp. 934-35.
[36]Ibid., p. 342.

oneself and others.[37] Rāmakrishna's followers became convinced that his visions were a manifestation of his sainthood and even incarnational status and that he was in continual touch with a supernatural realm normally inaccessible to ordinary mortals. As was noted with Rāmakrishna's madness, his visions allowed him certain liberties; he was free to act mad because his madness, from one perspective, was grounded in his visions and his quest for them.

Among American Indians, visions tended to enhance cohesion of social organizations.[38] This is also true for the community of followers gathered around the persona of Rāmakrishna. Individuals were attracted to this strange and mysterious man, who could suddenly leave the mundane realm and drift into another world and see wonderful things. In Rāmakrishna's case, there is a direct connection between his charisma and visions. His visions tended to reinforce and enhance his personal charismatic power.

If visions are commonly accepted as part of the religious system of belief by a group, they provide a rationale for explaining the differential distribution of power and prestige in a society. In other words, visions explain why certain individuals have a greater right to assume positions of prestige and privilege over others.[39] This social function of visions explains in part, at least, why no member of Rāmakrishna's entourage would ever think of challenging his leadership or preeminent position within the group. Rāmakrishna's followers were simply satisfied to be allowed to share his companionship. On the other hand, visions can be used to manipulate others. Although in the case of Rāmakrishna, his manipulation was rather subtle and non-threatening. Rāmakrishna possessed the ability, due to the aura associated with his saintliness, to motivate people without coercing them. Furthermore, as I. M. Lewis has demonstrated in his study of ecstatic cults, visions enable one to paradoxically escape from the confining bonds of society.[40] Thus, although visions can unify a group, they can also free the individual visionary of social bonds and their limitations.

Besides the Native American Indians and Rāmakrishna, visions also played a significant role in Christian mysticism and in other areas of Christian life and ideas. In his fascinating study entitled *The Birth of Purgatory*, Jacques Le Goff demonstrated that the visions of journeys to the afterworld and the subsequent tales of the souls of the dead receiving punishment in purgatory were important features helping to popularize the geography of the next world.[41] Since visions were considered genuine by the people of the Middle Ages, Le Goff cites their use by William of Auvergne to prove the reality of Purgatory.[42] Visions also played an important role in the life of St. Francis of Assisi. For instance, while in Rome at the Church of St. Peter, St. Francis prayed in one corner of the

---

[37]Albers and Parker, p. 205.

[38]Dugan, p. 171.

[39]Albers and Parker, p. 214.

[40]I. M. Lewis, *Ecstatic Religion: An Anthropological Study of Spirit Possession and Shamanism* (Middlesex: Penguin Books, Ltd., 1971), p. 127.

[41]Jacques Le Goff, *The Birth of Purgatory*, trans., Arthur Goldhammer (Chicago: University of Chicago Press, 1984), p. 177.

[42]Ibid., p. 243.

church for sometime until the apostles Peter and Paul appeared to him and informed him that his prayers were answered.[43] Later in life, St. Francis asked God for two graces: to feel in his body and soul the passion of Christ and to experience in his heart the love of Jesus. Subsequently, St. Francis saw a vision of a six winged, resplendent, burning seraph (Isa. 6:1-13) bearing a likeness between its wings to the crucified Christ.[44] This apparition resulted in the saint receiving on his body the famous stigmata, marks of Christ's passion. Although St. Francis' visionary adventures were recorded by his followers, many Christian mystics have recorded their visions in personal written accounts.

Few Christian mystics have recorded their visions more systematically than Julian of Norwich, who is an especially felicitous choice to examine because she, like Rāmakrishna, conceived of ultimate reality as a mother figure, at least as far as the second person of the Trinity for Julian. She summarized her conviction by stating, "And so Jesus is our true Mother in nature by our first creation, and he is our true Mother in grace by his taking our created nature."[45] The motherhood of Christ is dependent, according to Julian, on the resurrection after which He feeds us by means of the sacraments; He protects, heals, restores, and saves us by leading His children back to the Father.

An anchoress living beside a church in Norwich, England, Julian had her visionary experiences, a series of sixteen revelations, while she lay gravely ill on May 13, 1373. According to the longer version of the text, she wanted three graces: to see Christ's Passion; to attain bodily sickness; and to attain three wounds, that is, contrition, compassion and longing with her will for God. Why did she want bodily sickness? Her answer was to suffer with Christ, be purged by God's mercy, and to receive the reward of death in order to be with God.[46] During the thirtieth year of her life, she received the last rites of the church. After she had an experience of death as paralysis of her lower body, a priest set a cross before her. She then received her first vision or revelation.

Julian related the sight of red blood flowing from the crown upon Christ's head in this initial vision. In other visions she saw God in an instant of time (third revelation), the bleeding flesh of Christ (fourth revelation), God reigning as king in His house (sixth revelation), the passion of Christ (eight revelation), sin (thirteenth revelation), prayer (fourteenth revelation), a formless body from which a beautiful child sprang and ascended to heaven (fifteenth revelation). The sixteenth revelation was the last and confirmed the previous visions. Thus her visions were self-validating much like Rāmakrishna's visions. These sixteen revelations occurred while Julian was awake. When she fell asleep she had a vision of the devil, who tried to kill her but was unsuccessful. With each of her visions, the long version of the text implies that Julian received divinely inspired, often theologically sophisticated, interpretations of its meaning, which is a similar scenario in comparison to Rāmakrishna's understanding of his visions.

---

[43]St. Francis of Assisi, p. 35.

[44]Ibid., pp. 165-66.

[45]Julian of Norwich, *Showings*, trans., Edward Colledge, O.S.A. and James Walsh, S.J. (New York: Paulist Press, 1978), p. 296.

[46]Ibid., pp. 177-78.

The religious symbol system, of course, is completely different for both visionaries.

The vision quest among Native American Indians, Julian of Norwich and Rāmakrishna, as noted above, was often associated with periods of psychological stress. If a seeker was successful in acquiring a vision, this served to reduce anxieties connected to stressful, uncertain and dangerous situations.[47] The seeker gained personal confidence through his/her vision and mastery over his/her environment. Although there is no overwhelming evidence that Rāmakrishna was concerned with gaining mastery over his environment except indirectly, his visions gave him the confidence necessary to expound a message and convince him of the certainty of his religious inclinations.

Besides relieving the anxieties associated with dangerous situations, visions also reduce anxieties connected with one's newfound independence. In American Indian tribal societies, individuals are required to be brave, self-reliant, responsible and independent in order to be successful, even though one's identity is essentially defined socially. In order to ease the problem associated with assuming a heavier social and individual burden, a movement from a position of little responsibility to a transition of greater expectations, guardian spirits gained in visions served as protective parental surrogates for individual tribal members.[48] As Rāmakrishna slowly discovered his true identity, he was aided and comforted by his visions of Kālī, although he did not appear to desire any independence from the Goddess.

VISIONS AND PLAY

Numerous differences and similarities between Native American Indians, Julian of Norwich and Rāmakrishna have been observed with relation to their visions and the quest for such visual experiences. With relation to some major differences, it has been noted that Rāmakrishna's visions were often continual, could arise by means of an innocent trigger mechanism and became more sublime or more abstract as one advanced spiritually. But the major difference between the visions of Rāmakrishna, American Indians and Julian of Norwich was the playful nature of the former's experiences. There is little or no evidence to suggest that American Indians understood their visions in terms of play. And Julian of Norwich's visions were more closely associated with pain and suffering.

After his vision of non-dual consciousness referred to above and his informing M about its contents, Rāmakrishna asked M what he thought, and the latter replied that the Goddess sported through the Master.[49] Although the Goddess was ultimately formless, she also possessed many forms by which she revealed herself to her devotees. Rāmakrishna related that he saw her in a yellow colored

---

[47]Anthony F. C. Wallace, *Religion: An Anthropological Viewpoint* (New York: Random House, 1966), p. 175.

[48]See Ruth Benedict, *The Concept of the Guardian Spirit in North America* (Menasha, Wisconsin: Memoirs of the American Anthropological Association, 1923).

[49]M, p. 282.

garment and spoke to her. Another time she appeared to him as a young, naked Muslim girl with a *tilak* mark on her forehead. The Master and young girl walked together, joking, playing and enjoying each other.[50] This episode demonstrates a direct link between play and visions in the mind of Rāmakrishna. Thus he concurred with M's statement that the Goddess sported through him and with him.

To have a vision with one's own eyes or mentally is to gain lucidity and certainty. Thus to see something is to know it or to be certain of it because in the traditional Hindu context the eye is directly related to truth.[51] For Rāmakrishna, it is the truth of Kālī's presence and playfulness.

By means of his visions, Rāmakrishna—the seer—received a view *(darśan)* of Kālī, the object of his vision. Referring to the Hindi term for *darśan,* Hawley notes that it includes the action of seeing, the sight itself, and can include, if the object of vision is fascinating enough, a submerging of the seer in that which is seen.[52] The merging of Rāmakrishna and the object of his sight was certainly a common occurrence in his visionary experiences. Therefore, Rāmakrishna's visions dissolved the distance between himself and the object of his desires. Distance was erased in two senses: an outer distance dissolved by the eye and an internal distance overcome by the mind. The outer and internal distances created by a normal mind and eye were overcome by Rāmakrishna when absorbed in a vision of Kālī.

With the eradication of spacial barriers, Rāmakrishna could enter into play without any hindrance normally associated with separation created by distance. By bridging the distance gap between himself and his playmate through his visions, Rāmakrishna was able to establish contact with his beloved. Not only does seeing form contact with an object, it is also, as Gonda notes in ancient Indian thought, a form of touching.[53] By means of his seeing, Rāmakrishna was able to transform himself by drinking with his eyes the divine power of the Goddess. On the other hand, the Goddess also saw Rāmakrishna, establishing a special sort of intimacy between the two parties in the game of sight. If the Goddess is an object of Rāmakrishna's sight, and if he is an object of her sight, Rāmakrishna was able to participate in Kālī's being by uniting her seeing with his own. Thus participation in the game of seeing enabled Rāmakrishna to know the Goddess and to know himself in a new way.[54] Therefore, Rāmakrishna was able to enter into a very intimate, playful relationship with Kālī by means of his visions. He could see, know, touch and play with her.

We have seen that Rāmakrishna enjoyed his visions while in a state of *samādhi* (absorption). Rāmakrishna distinguished between two kinds of *samādhi: sthira* or *jada* and *bhāva.* The seeker attained the former type of *samādhi* by fol-

---

[50]Ibid., p. 175.

[51]Cited by J. Gonda, *Eye and Gaze in the Veda* (Amsterdam: North-Holland Publishing Company, 1969), p. 9.

[52]Hawley, *Krishna, The Butter Thief,* p. 105.

[53]Gonda, *Eye and Gaze,* p. 19.

[54]Lawrence A. Babb, "Glancing: Visual Interaction in Hinduism," *Journal of Anthropological Research,* Vol. 37 (1981), p. 397.

lowing the path of knowledge, which entailed the destruction of the ego. In contrast, *bhāva samādhi* is gained by pursuing the path of *bhakti* (devotion). With relation to the play of the Goddess, the second type of *samādhi* was to be preferred because in this type of *samādhi* a trace of ego remained in the individual.[55] It was this remnant of ego which made enjoyment of one's visions and the play of the Goddess possible. In fact, it was the Goddess herself who kept a trace of ego in her devotee not merely for enjoyment but also to enable the lover to work for the welfare of humanity. Although an individual's trace of ego allowed one to enjoy the play *(līlā)* of the Goddess, it must not be confused with the ultimate source of the visions, which depended on the gratuitous grace of the Divine Mother.[56] Before grace was given, it was necessary to have a longing in one's heart for the Goddess. Thus Rāmakrishna did not want to assert that an individual must be simply a passive recipient and have nothing to do. However, the ultimate decision to enter into play and give the gift of visions rested with Kālī, the merciful, loving, mother figure.

In comparison to Rāmakrishna, Caitanya, the sixteenth-century Bengali saint, found his visions not to be as enjoyable. As Caitanya sleep one night, he saw a vision of Krishna playing in the *rāsa-līlā* (circle dance) with his flute in his mouth, wearing golden garments and a garland of woodland flowers. The *gopīs* danced in an unbroken circle and in the middle danced Krishna with Rādhā. When Caitanya awoke he was sad that it was only a vision.[57] Rāmakrishna appeared to receive some emotional and mental relief from his visions, whereas Caitanya did not.

As we have implied, the visions received by Rāmakrishna throughout his adult life are another example of the play *(līlā)* of Kālī. The visions of Rāmakrishna set him apart, like a stranger and madman, from the rest of Hindus. Rāmakrishna was the lucky recipient of the gifts of the Goddess in the form of wonderful visions. These visions, grounded in Kālī's grace, were part of the drama directed by the Goddess through the person of Rāmakrishna, her leading actor in the divine drama enacted for the most part on the outskirts of Calcutta.

Like playful gifts, these visions were an end in themselves. They were a free gift, intentionless in character, spontaneously given, and unpredictable in their content. The visions of Rāmakrishna are another indication of his unconditioned freedom and liberation from worldly bondage. In his book on shamanism, Eliade asserts that seeing a divine spirit, either in a dream or awake, implies that one has obtained a spiritual condition, a transcending of the profane condition of humanity.[58] Moreover, Rāmakrishna's visions are indicative of the grace of the Goddess and his absorption in Kālī to the exclusion of everything mundane.

According to the biography of Sāradā Devī, the wife of Rāmakrishna, written by Swami Gambhirānanda, the Master appeared to her in visions after his death. A vision of Rāmakrishna occurred on the banks of the Ganges when the

---

[55]M, p. 812.

[56]Ibid., p. 646.

[57]C. C., III.14.15-21.

[58]Mircea Eliade, *Shamanism: Archaic Techniques of Ecstasy,* trans. Willard R. Trask (New York: Pantheon Books, 1964), p. 85.

spirit of her departed husband emerged from behind and rushed passed her into the river. She reported that his spiritual body dissolved in the holy waters, leaving her dumbfounded. The vividness of the vision caused Sāradā Devī to refrain from bathing in the Ganges for fear of stepping on Rāmakrishna's body.[59] On another occasion Rāmakrishna appeared to his wife and asked her to feed him.[60] Thus, according to his followers, Rāmakrishna continued to play after his death with his wife through visions just as Kālī appeared to him during his life.

During her life, Sāradā Devī, the child-bride of Rāmakrishna, also received visions of Kālī, according to her biographer. While suffering from a high fever, she saw a dark woman of peerless beauty, who caressed her feverish head with soft, cool hands and helped her recover from her illness.[61] Another vision occurred near the time of Rāmakrishna's death. Sāradā Devī reported that she saw Kālī in a dream, who indicated to her that the Goddess also had cancer of the throat just like Rāmakrishna.[62] This is clear evidence of a dream reflecting reality. It is, of course, true that Indian dreams can also cause reality.[63]

Due to the void created by the death of Rāmakrishna and the significance of visions in his life, the fellowship that evolved around him during his life needed someone to fill the gap created by his departure. The members of the fellowship needed a new focus upon which to direct their *guru*-devotion. Sāradā Devī or the Divine Mother, as she was called by the devotees, filled the void. If this scenario is combined with the conviction in the incarnational nature of Rāmakrishna by his followers, the visions attributed to Sāradā Devī make perfect sense and are consistent with the expectations of the members of the devotional fellowship.

---

[59]Gambhirananda, p. 174.
[60]Ibid., p. 154.
[61]Ibid., p. 42.
[62]Ibid., p. 135.
[63]O'Flaherty, *Dreams*, p. 19.

Chapter VIII

CONCLUSION

Just as the nature of the black Goddess represents a coincidence of various opposites—creativity and destructiveness, threatening and forgiving, vengeful and loving, ferocious and gracious—the mysterious play of Kālī demonstrates, as shown in the previous chapters, that the world that she created is a combination of joy and sorrow, good and evil, and a place of bondage and a nexus of liberation. Likewise, the life of the leading player in Kālī's drama—Rāmakrishna—experienced the joy of fellowship and the suffering associated with separation from human and divine loved ones, humor and tragedy, divine visions and unawareness of the historical and cultural changes that were occurring about him. But the world and every joy and sorrow that it represented was all a grandiose illusion created by Kālī. If one could see it for what it was, then, the groping for liberation or the attempt to discover one's destiny within the grand illusion was fun. Despite the pain and sorrow, one could still dance, sing and laugh. Thus Rāmakrishna heroically affirmed human existence by his life in spite of suffering within the *māyā* of Kālī.

The mysterious aspect of Kālī's dramatic production centered in part on her actions and on those of her leading male actor who was a complex and contradictory figure. We have seen that Rāmakrishna was a fully human bundle of contradictions. He appeared to harbor, for instance, a latent misogynist attitude, yet he was an ardent devotee of Kālī and perceived women positively as manifestations of the Goddess. Even though his overall perception of women was generally negative, Rāmakrishna occasionally assumed the dress and demeanor of females. He appeared to be confused about his own sexuality. He fluctuated between trance absorption and normal states of consciousness, or he laughed one moment and cried profusely the next. He carried on conversations with his followers and invisible beings. He practiced and advocated various forms of *bhakti,* Tantra, Advaita Vedānta, Islam, and Christianity, which are hardly compatible religious paths. According to the script enacted by Rāmakrishna, periods of activity were punctuated by moments of immobility, mental lucidity followed by confusion or vice versa, and periods of depression succeeded by joy. Although there were often wide mood, mental and physical swings in his life, these striking changes manifested a very vulnerable human being.

Apparently, Rāmakrishna was oblivious to and unaffected by the multitude of economic, social, political and intellectual changes swirling around him. It was as if Rāmakrishna represented the timeless, unchanging hub of a wheel whose outer rim was ever turning and changing. In a sense, either as a traditional Indian saint or incarnation, depending on one's perspective, Rāmakrishna represented a symbolic thread of continuity with the Hindu past and a source of stability within the flux and challenges offered by nineteenth-century Calcutta. If Rāmakrishna was removed from the influence of the changing historical mainstream, he was not divorced from the central focus of the Indian religious tradition. Even though he was a bit eclectic in his religious thinking, he was from one perspective a Hindu to the very core of his being. He represented an ancient figure in modern times, a juxtaposition of the old and new.

From another perspective, Rāmakrishna was in historical time, but out of place. It was as if he were a museum artifact, a remnant of India's religious past, rediscovered in the changing nineteenth century. His behavior leads one to believe that he lived mentally and spiritually in a changeless, cosmic space and time beyond the flux and confinement of modern history. He still, however, embodied a centuries old message: seek the truth. For many people, Rāmakrishna was a link to the traditional Hindu penchant for venerating saints. If Rāmakrishna was a link to the Hindu religious past and a form of its continuity, his own life was united by the thread of the continual play of Kālī which was at times enlightening, humorous, strange, painful and enjoyable.

Even though he was a bundle of contradictions and a complex figure, the pure, spontaneous, unpredictable and purposeless play of Kālī united the incidents in Rāmakrishna's life into a loving whole. Rāmakrishna obviously enjoyed playing with the Goddess, being her plaything and playing with his followers. Just as Kālī controlled the game that she purposelessly played with Rāmakrishna, in turn, he was in command with his followers and playmates, even though he personally appeared to be unable to control himself at times. Whether investigating the play of Kālī with Rāmakrishna or with his followers, the essence of either playful relationship is always love. While frolicking with Kālī and assuming the leading male part in her mysterious drama, Rāmakrishna played numerous roles: dancer; child; woman; madman; humorist; stranger; and recipient of visions.

Like a puppet dangling on a string controlled by the master puppeteer named Kālī, Rāmakrishna would dance and sing when intoxicated with the ecstasy of divine love, overflowing with emotion, forgetting the world and losing himself in the inundation of bliss. His singing and dancing suggested a spirit of renunciation because he was transported to a realm of bliss and love within this world but pointing beyond the mundane realm. The mood created by Rāmakrishna's singing, dancing and love-intoxicated condition was contagious and an invitation for others to join in his revelry.

Besides giving a convincing and award-winning performance as a woman and assuming the feminine devotional mood, which suggested that the male and female sexual roles were transferable within the realm of play, Rāmakrishna also played the role of a child in an adult male's body. From his early childhood when he assumed the roles of divine beings in village theatrical productions to his adulthood when he accepted the part of saint or divine incarnation, he was a child who never stopped playing. Rāmakrishna never assumed any significant measure of adult responsibility. Because of his odd behavior and sudden trance states, he needed others to care for him, much like children need mothers who assume the responsibility for their care. Thus he retained the innocence of an irresponsible child throughout his life, which proved to be an opportunity for extended fun, games and enjoyment, free of the limitations imposed by the drugery of work.

A more prominent role played by Rāmakrishna was that of a madman, not only for Kālī, but also for a variety of Hindu deities. As a *gopī* or Rādhā, he was mad for Krishna. For the divine Rāma, he assumed the role of Hanumān or manifested madness for the child Rāma (Rāmalala), which was referred to as *pūjā* madness. As a substitute for the *liṅga* of Śiva, Rāmakrishna worshiped his own penis. But overall his madness was grounded in the madness for Kālī. In fact, he asked the mad mistress for the gift of madness in order for her to play with him on the stage of the world.

Always wanting his beloved Goddess near him and desiring to see and touch her, Rāmakrishna was driven mad when he and Kālī were physically separated. Rāmakrishna was driven to the brink of committing suicide by the madness generated by his separation from his beloved immortal.

From one perspective, Rāmakrishna's bizarre behavior suggested that he was a mental and social misfit. But if we place his odd actions within the religious tradition of devotional Hinduism and within the context of his own devotion to Kālī, his madness was a manifestation and celebration of his spiritual freedom and a gracious gift from the Goddess of death and destruction. This radical freedom was the type that called the absurdities of life into question and broke down the distinction between sane and insane and other dichotomies. The gift of madness was accompanied by spiritual insight into the true nature of this madhouse of a world, a chance product of a mad Goddess. The gratuitous gift of madness also gave Rāmakrishna the insight that enabled him to perceive everything as Kālī.

In order to survive, thrive, sing, dance, teach, laugh and play, it was necessary to become mad. This entailed, however, an existential risk because Rāmakrishna was always on the physical, emotional and mental brink. Yet he was ready to venture his well being for that which he perceived to be permanent and beyond the confines of the madness of the ephemeral world. This spiritual gambler was a model for religious liberation, and the type of person who would jump at the opportunity to take the wager of Blaise Pascal. There was something magnetic about the madness of the religious daredevil that attracted others to the overt manifestation of his saintliness.

The madman was not without his sense of humor. Although Rāmakrishna shared some common features with the fool, clown and trickster, he was closer to the figure of a comedian based in the world and the absurdities of the human condition yet able to transcend these limitations and perceive the truth; yet he was able to do this without forgetting to affirm the sacredness and worth of life. As the comedian of the Goddess, the goals of Rāmakrishna were to liberate human beings from their spiritual wasteland, to conquer dualities, to unite human beings in a loving fellowship and with the only reality.

Grounded in his faith, the various types of humor manifested by Rāmakrishna gave him courage and certainty. There was a suggestion that his humorous anecdotes were intended to make others examine and evaluate themselves. If one possessed the comic perception of the absurdity of certain human situations, Rāmakrishna was suggesting that this would open the possibility for deeper insights into the human condition. Or the perception of the incongruity of a situation allowed one to disengage oneself from it and to gain a distance from it. Rāmakrishna's humorous stories also called his followers to use their imaginations and to allow their creative faculties and energy to overflow. There was also a less intentionless and less serious aspect of his humor. The humor of Rāmakrishna also suggested the enjoyment and purposelessness of play. Humor was a playful path for Rāmakrishna that liberated those who were able to laugh. Those who were overly somber and serious were caught in a state of bondage unable to see into humorous aspects of human deficiencies, the mistaking of one thing for another, the happenstance of coincidence and the often hilarious juxtaposition of opposites. As a form of play, humor is shared with others without any real goal or purpose. It enabled Rāmakrishna and his followers to share in something irrational and frivolous, to enter into a voluntary activity, and to renew and refresh themselves. Unlike the ever serious person, Rāmakrishna was able to laugh at his own foolishness, at the folly of others and the nonsense of the world, which detached and liberated him from his own self-delusions and the binding power of the world. The humorous side of Rāmakrishna's role was more easy for his associates to comprehend because it was a human quality they could all enjoy sharing with their master, but his part as the stranger left them wondering and uncomfortable.

Just as Kālī bewildered him, Rāmakrishna mystified those that he encountered throughout his life. He was certainly the mystery within the mysterious play of Kālī. Through the eyes of M and other intimate followers, we were able in the sixth chapter to view Rāmakrishna as a stranger, a person who called basic assumptions into question and thereby created uneasiness, a threatening figure who was unpredictable, and one who tested the religious culture and discovered its validity by personal experience. Even though Rāmakrishna was probably not a stranger to the members of Hindu culture in his own mind, those that he encountered were confounded and astonished by his behavior. They were particularly uncertain when the possibility arose that Rāmakrishna, an earthly alien, might be a divine incarnation, a stranger to human beings by definition. Rāmakrishna fulfilled the role of a stranger for those that he encountered because of the difficulty involved in recognizing an incarnation, which represented an aberration, a coincidence of opposites or an absurdity. In his role as a stranger, Rāmakrishna played the part of the mysterious, itinerant pilgrim on the surface of the earth.

And the primary reason for the incarnation, although some other reasons were given in chapter six, was simply an excuse to play. In other words, through the person of Rāmakrishna, Kālī was able to play with her creatures. Thus Rāmakrishna, as the stranger, brought divine play *(līlā)* to earth, creating a heavenly realm on earth and giving ordinary mortals a foretaste of divine bliss. The mortal players were wrenched free from the security of their accepted and unquestioned ways and invited to join the fun of the game. Once one participated in the game, one found oneself also in a process of redefining and rediscovering one's true identity, which was a joyous experience. Thus the stranger was a spoiler because after encountering him and joining his game, nothing would ever be the same again.

A feature of Rāmakrishna's nature that made him appear strange to others was his visions, an inward sign of his holiness. Not a psychotic fantasy, his visions had a cultural meaning because they were expressed in an accepted religious idiom and common cultural symbols. Many visions were spontaneous and ended feelings of separation from Kālī. Thereby, they relieved his emotional and mental anguish, and they informed us that the closer one spiritually advanced toward Kālī the less gross or embodied became one's visions of the divine. Although Rāmakrishna's visions were expressed in culturally comprehensible ways, they were personal and not originally the property of his culture. Of course, his visions were claimed by the Hindu culture once they were shared by Rāmakrishna with others and recorded for future generations.

From his visions of Kālī and other divine beings, Rāmakrishna received advice, messages or cures. Not only were his visions a suggestion that he was in continual touch with a transcendent being, his visions also enhanced social cohesion within Rāmakrishna's fellowship and gave him power and prestige within the group, adding even more to his personal charisma and influence over his followers. In a more personal way, Rāmakrishna's visions gave him religious certainty and the confidence necessary to expound his message.

In a sense, Rāmakrishna's madness was grounded in his visions and his quest for them. Moreover, his visions were an indication that the Goddess sported through him. As long as a trace of ego remained in him, Rāmakrishna was able to play a kind of perceptual game with Kālī in which he could also know, touch and play with her. Intentionless in character, spontaneously given and unpredictable in their content, the visions of Rāmakrishna were a free gift and indicative of the grace of Kālī. These gratuitous gifts enabled Rāmakrishna to dissolve the distance between himself and his Goddess and allowed him to enter into play with Kālī and other deities. Absorbed in play with Kālī and other deities, Rāmakrishna manifested unconditioned freedom unbounded by spacial barriers. Like his role as the stranger and madman, his visions set him apart from others.

With the death of Rāmakrishna, the dramatic play produced and directed by Kālī came to a conclusion. Although Rāmakrishna inspired a religious movement that was developed and spread by his devoted followers, the activity of Kālī slowly waned in the life of the religious fellowship and the Goddess was shoved into the background to become a minor player and not the primary focus of attention as she was for Rāmakrishna. Why was Kālī not emphasized by Rāmakrishna's followers? Why did she fail to play a central role in the movement guided by Swami Vivekānanda? For Vivekānanda and other members of the Rāmakrishna Math and Mission, Kālī seemed to be an embarrassment to their more intellectual proclivities and tastes. Therefore, the nature and appearance of the frightening, gruesome, blood thirsty Goddess was not something that would play well on the stage of the late nineteenth and early twentieth centuries in India nor western countries. And the strong devotional attitude of Rāmakrishna towards his beloved Goddess was also neglected. The play had to be revised and censored in parts for modern theatrical tastes and sensibilities. The emphasis would now be concentrated on Brahman and the intellectually more refined and satisfying Advaita Vedānta philosophy. Kālī was forced to adjourn to the recesses of her temple, a rest-home for retired, divine performers past their prime.

BIBLIOGAPHY

Abbott, Justin E., trans. *Life of Tukaram translation from Mahipati's Bhakta-lilamrita, Chapters 25 to 40.* Delhi: Motilal Banarsidass, 1980.

Albers, Patricia and Parker, Seymour. "The Plains Vision Experience: A Study of Power and Privilege." *Southwestern Journal of Anthropology.* 27, 3 (Autumn 1971): 203-233.

Alderman, Harold. "The Place of Comedy." *Man and World: An International Philosophical Review* 10 (1977): 152-172.

Alston, A. J., trans. *The Devotional Poems of Mīrābāī.* Delhi: Motilal Banarsidass, 1980.

Arberry, A. J., trans. *Muslim Saints and Mystics.* Chicago: University of Chicago Press, 1966.

Babb, Lawrence A. "Glancing: Visual Interaction in Hinduism." *Journal of Anthropological Research.* 37 (1981): 387-401.

Benedict, Ruth. *The Concept of the Guardian Spirit in North America.* Memoirs of the American Anthropological Association. Menasha, Wisconsin, 1923.

________. "The Vision in Plains Culture." *American Anthropologist* 24, no. 1 January-March 1922): 1-23.

The Bhāgavata Purāṇa. Translated by Ganesh Vasudeo Tagare. 5 vols. Delhi: Motilal Banarsidass, 1976.

Bhoosnurmath, S. S. and Menezes, Armando, trans. *Śūnyasaṁpādane* Vol. IV. Dharwar: Karnatak University, 1970.

Brown, C. Mackenzie. "Kālī, the Mad Mother." In Carl Olson, ed. *The Book of the Goddess Past and Present: An Introduction to Her Religion.* New York: Crossroad Publishing Company, 1983, pp. 110-123.

Brown, Joseph Epes. *The Sacred Pipe: Black Elk's Account of the Seven Rites of the Oglala Sioux.* Baltimore: Penguin Books, 1979.

Caillois, Roger. *Man, Play, and Games.* Translated by Meyer Barash. New York: The Free Press, 1961.

Caitanya-caritāmṛta of Kṛṣṇadāsa Kavirāja Edited with the commentary Gaurā-kṛpa-taraṇgini by Rādhāgovinda Nath. 6 vols. Calcutta: Bhakti-pracanabhanden, 1949-1950.

Camus, Albert. *The Stranger.* Translated by Stuart Gilbert. New York: A. A. Knopf, 1951.

Coomaraswamy, Ananda K. *The Dance of Siva.* New Delhi: Sagar Publications, 1971. .

_______. "Līlā." *Journal of the American Oriental Society* 61 (1941): 98-101.

Cox, Harvey. *The Feast of Fools: A Theological Essay on Festivity and Fantasy.* Cambridge: Harvard University Press, 1969.

Crumrine, N. Ross. "Čapakoba, The Mayo Easter Ceremonial Impersonator: Explanations of Ritual Clowning." *Journal for the Scientific Study of Religion* 8, no. 1 (Spring 1969): 1-22.

Diagnostic and Statistical Manual of Mental Disorders. Third Edition. Washington, D. C: American Psychiatric Association, 1980.

Dimock, Edward C. Jr. *The Place of the Hidden Moon: Erotic Mysticism in the Vaiṣṇava-Sahajiyā Cult of Bengal.* Chicago: University of Chicago Press, 1966. .

_______. "Religious Biography in India: The 'Nectar of the Acts' of Caitanya." In Frank E. Reynolds and Donald Capps, eds. *The Biographical Process: Studies in the History and Psychology of Religion.* The Hague: Mouton, 1976, pp. 109-117.

Douglas, Mary. "The Social Control of Cognition: Some Factors in Joke Perception." *Man* 3 (1968): 361-376.

Dugan, Kathleen Margaret. *The Vision Quest of the Plains Indians: Its Spiritual Significance.* Studies in American Religion Vol. 13. Lewiston/Queenston: Edwin Mellen Press, 1985.

Eck, Diana L. *Darśan, Seeing the Divine Image in India.* Chambersburg, PA: Anima Books, 1981. .

_______. "India's Tīrthas: 'Crossing' in Sacred Geography." *History of Religions* 20, no. 4 (May 1981): 323-344.

Eidlitz, Walther. *Kṛṣṇa-Caitanya Sein Leben und Seine Lehre.* Stockholm Studies in Comparative Religion 7. Stockholm: Almquist and Wiksell, 1968.

Eliade, Mircea. *Shamanism: Archaic Techniques of Ecstasy.* Translated by Willard R. Trask. New York: Pantheon Books, 1964. .

________. *Yoga: Immortality and Freedom.* Translated by Willard R. Trask. Second Edition. Princeton: Princeton University Press, 1969.

Feldhaus, Anne, trans. *The Deeds of God in Ṛddhipur.* New York: Oxford University Press, 1984.

Fraser, J. Nelson and Marathe, K. B. eds. and trans. *The Poems of Tukārāma* 3 Vols. Madras: The Christian Literature Society, 1909, 1913, 1915.

French, Harold W. *The Swan's Wide Waters: Ramakrishna and Western Culture.* Port Washington, N.Y: Kennikat Press, 1974.

Gadamer, Hans-Georg. *Truth and Method.* Translated by Garrett Barden and John Cumming. New York: Crossroad Publishing Company, 1982.

Gambhirananda, Swami. *Holy Mother Shri Sarada Devi.* Madras: Sri Ramakrishna Math, 1955.

Ghosh, Manomohan, trans. *The Nāṭyaśāstra.* Vol. 1. Second Edition. Calcutta: Granthalaya Private Limited, 1967.

Gonda, J. *Eye and Gaze in the Veda.* Amsterdam-London: North-Holland Publishing Company, 1969. .

________. *Die Religionen Indiens: II Der jüngere Hinduismus.* Stuttgart: W. Kohlhammer Verlag, 1963.

Handelman, Don. "The Ritual-Clown: Attributes and Affinities." *Anthropos* 76 (1981): 321-370.

Hardy, Friedhelm. *Viraha-Bhakti: The Early History of Kṛṣṇa Devotion in South India.* Delhi: Oxford University Press, 1983.

Hartt, Julian N. *The Restless Quest.* Philadelphia: United Church Press, 1975.

Hawley, John Stratton. *At Play with Krishna: Pilgrimage Dramas from Brindavan.* Princeton: Princeton University Press, 1981. .

Krishna, The Butter Thief. Princeton: Princeton University Press, 1983.

Heywood, W. trans. *The Little Flowers of the Glorious Messer St. Francis and of His Friars*. Second Edition. London: Methuen & Company, Ltd., 1924.

Holmer, Paul. "Something About What Makes It Funny." *Soundings* LXII, no. 2 (Summer 1974): 157-174.

Huizinga, Johan. *Homo Ludens: A Study of the Play-Element in Culture*. Boston: Beacon Press, 1955.

Hyers, M. Conrad. "The Comic Profanation of the Sacred." In *Holy Laughter: Essays on Religion in the Comic Perspective*. Edited by M. Conrad Hyers. New York: Seabury Press, 1969, pp. 9-27. .

_______. *The Comic Vision and the Christian Faith: A Celebration of Life and Laughter*. New York: Pilgrim Press, 1981.

Ingalls, Daniel H. H. "Cynics and Pāśupatas: The Seeking of Dishonor." *Harvard Theological Review* LV (1962): 281-298.

Isherwood, Christopher. *Ramakrishna and His Disciples*. New York: Simon and Schuster, 1965

Julian of Norwich. *Showings*. Translated by Edmund Colledge, O.S.A. and James Walsh, S.J. New York: Paulist Press, 1978.

Keith, A. Berriedale. *The Sanskrit Drama in Its Origin, Development, Theory and Practice*. London: Oxford University Press, 1924; reprint ed., 1970.

Kennedy, Melville T. *The Chaitanya Movement: A Study of the Vaishavism of Bengal*. Calcutta: Association Press, 1925.

Kinsley, David R. The Sword and the Flute: *Kālī and Kṛṣṇa, Dark Visions of the Terrible and Sublime in Hindu Mythology*. Berkeley: University of California Press, 1975. .

_______. "'Through the Looking Glass': Divine Madness in the Hindu Religious Tradition." *History of Religions* 13, no. 4 (May 1974): 270-305.

_______. "Without Kṛṣṇa There Is No Song." *History of Religions* 12, no. 2 (November 1972): 149-180.

Kopf, David. *The Brahmo Samaj and the Shaping of the Modern Indian Mind*. Princeton: Princeton University Press, 1979. .

_______. *British Orientalism and the Bengal Renaissance: The Dynamics of Indian Modernization 1773-1835*. Berkeley: University of California Press, 1969.

Kramrisch, Stella. *The Presence of Śiva*. Princeton: Princeton University Press, 1981

Laing, R. D. *The Divided Self*. London: Tavistock, 1959. .

_______. *The Politics of Experience*. New York: Pantheon Books, 1967. .

_______. *The Self and Others*. London: Tavistock, 1961.

Lange, Charles. *Cochiti*. Carbondale: Southern Illinois University Press, 1968.

Lauter, Paul ed. *Theories of Comedy*. Garden City, N.Y: Doubleday and Company, Inc., 1964.

Le Goff, Jacques. *The Birth of Purgatory*. Translated by Arthur Goldhammer. Chicago: University of Chicago Press, 1984.

Lemaitre, Solange. *Ramakrishna and the Vitality of Hinduism*. Translated by Charles Lam Markmann. New York: Funk and Wagnalls, 1969.

Lewis, I. M. *Ecstatic Religion: An Anthropological Study of Spirit Possession and Shamanism*. Middlesex: Penguin Books, Ltd., 1971.

Life of Sri Ramakrishna. Tenth Impression. Calcutta: Advaita Ashrama, 1977.

The Liṅga Purāṇa. 2 Vols. Translated by A Board of Scholars. Delhi: Motilal Banarsidass, 1973.

Lorenzen, David N. *The Kāpālikas and Kālāmukhas: Two Lost Śaivite Sects*. Berkeley: University of California Press, 1972.

M. *The Gospel of Sri Ramakrishna*. Translated by Swami Nikhilananda. New York: Ramakrishna-Vivekananda Center, 1973.

McHugh, Paul R. and Slavney, Phillip R. *The Perspectives of Psychiatry*. Baltimore and London: The Johns Hopkins University Press, 1983.

Makarius, Laura. "Ritual Clowns and Symbolic Behaviour." *Diogenes* 69 (1970): 44-73

Mandel, Oscar. "What So Funny: The Nature of the Comic." *The Antioch Review* 30 (Spring 1970): 73-89.

Martin, Mike W. "Humour and Aesthetic Enjoyment of Incongruities." *British Journal of Aesthetics* 23, no. 1 (Winter 1983): 74-85.

Matchett, Freda. "The Teaching of Rāmakrishna in Religion to the Hindu Tradition and as Interpreted by Vivekānanda." *Religion* 11 (1981): 171-184.

Matsya Purāṇa. Ānandāśrama Sanskrit Series 54. Poona, 1907.

Morinis, E. Alan. *Pilgrimage in the Hindu Tradition: A Case Study of West Bengal.* Delhi: Oxford University Press, 1984.

Morreall, John. *Taking Laughter Seriously.* Albany: State University of New York Press, 1983.

Muller, F. Max. *Ramakrishna His Life and Sayings.* Mayavati: Advaita Ashram, 1951. .

_______. *Rammohan to Ramakrishna.* Calcutta: Susil Gupta (India) Ltd., 1952.

Neevel, Walter G. Jr. "The Transformation of Śrī Rāmakrishna." In Bardwell L. Smith ed. *Hinduism: New Essays in the History of Religions.* Leiden: E. J. Brill, 1976; reprint 1982, pp. 53-97.

Nehru, Jawaharlal. *Toward Freedom: Autobiography.* Boston: Beacon Press, 1958.

Neihardt, John G. *Black Elk Speaks.* New York: Washington Square Press, 1972.

Obeyesekere, Gananath. *The Cult of the Goddess Pattini.* Chicago: University of Chicago Press, 1984. .

_______. Medusa's Hair: *An Essay on Personal Symbols and Religious Experience.* Chicago and London: University of Chicago Press, 1981.

O'Flaherty, Wendy Doniger. *Dreams, Illusions, and other Realities.* Chicago: University of Chicago Press, 1984. .

_______. *Women, Androgynes, and Other Mythical Beasts.* Chicago and London: University of Chicago Press, 1980.

Olson, Carl. "Śrī Lakshmī and Rādhā: The Obsequious Wife and the Lustful Lover." In Carl Olson ed. *The Book of the Goddess Past and Present: An Introduction to Her Religion.* New York: Crossroad Publishing Company, 1983, pp. 124-144.

Opler, Morris Edward. *An Apache Life-Way.* New York: Cooper Square Publishers, Inc., 1965.

Östör, Ákos. *The Play of the Gods.* Chicago and London: University of Chicago Press, 1980.

Pandey, S. M. "Mīrābāī and Her Contributions to the Bhakti Movement" *History of Religions* 5, no. 1 (Summer 1965): 54-73.

Pangborn, Cyrus R. "The Rāmakrishna Math and Mission: A Case Study of a Revitalization Movement." In Bardwell L. Smith ed. *Hinduism: New Essays in the History of Religions.* Leiden: E. J. Brill, 1976; reprint 1982, pp. 98-119.

Pargiter, F. E. trans. *The Mārkaṇḍeya Purāṇa.* Calcutta: The Asiatic Society, 1904.; reprint Delhi and Varanasi: Indological Book House, 1969.

Parsons, Elsie Clews and Beals, Ralph L. "The Sacred Clowns of the Pueblo and Mayo-Yaqui Indians." *American Anthropologist* 36,4 (October-December 1934): 491-514.

Pelton, Robert D. *The Trickster in West Africa: A Study of Mythic Irony and Sacred Delight.* Berkeley: University of California Press, 1980.

Pope, G. U., trans. *The Tiruvāsagam of Mānikka-Vāsagar.* Oxford: Clarendon Press, 1900.

Powers, William K. *Oglala Religion.* Lincoln: University of Nebraska Press, 1977. .

_______. *Yuwipi, Vision and Experience in Oglala Ritual.* Lincoln: University of Nebraska Press, 1982.

Radin, P. *The Trickster: A Study in American Indian Mythology.* New York: Philosophical Library, 1956.

Ramanujan, A. K., trans. *Hymns for the Drowning: Poems for Viṣṇu by Nammāḷvār.* Princeton: Princeton University Press, 1981. .

_______. trans. *Speaking of Śiva.* Baltimore: Penguin Books, Inc., 1973.

Ranade, R. D. *Mysticism in India: The Poet-Saints of Maharashtra.* Albany: State University of New York Press, 1983; reprint of *Indian Mysticism: Mysticism in Maharashtra,* 1933.

Rangacharya, Adya. *Introduction to Bharata's Nāṭya-Śāstra*. Bombay: Popular Prakashan, 1966.

Ricketts, Mac Linscott. "The North American Trickster." *History of Religions* 5, no. 4 (1966): 327-350.

Rolland, Romain. *The Life of Ramakrishna*. Translated by E. F. Malcolm-Smith. Calcutta: Advaita Ashrama, 1979.

Roy, Manishna. *Bengali Women*. Chicago and London: University of Chicago Press, 1975.

Sanford, James. *Zen-Man Ikkyū*. Studies in World Religions 2. Chico, CA: Scholars Press, 1981.

Saradananda, Swami. *Sri Ramakrishna The Great Master*. 2 Vols. Translated by Swami Jagadananda. Fifth Edition. Madras: Sri Ramakrishna Math, 1978, 1979.

Saward, John. *Perfect Fools: Folly for Christ's Sake in Catholic and Orthodox Spirituality*. Oxford University Press, 1980.

Schneiderman, Leo. "Ramakrishna: Personality and Social Factors in the Growth of a Religious Movement." *Journal for the Scientific Study of Religion*. 8 (Spring 1969): 60-71.

Schreiner, Peter. "Sri Ramakrishna und Ramana Maharshi als Vertreter moderner indischer Mystik." In *Rausch-Ekstase-Mystik: Grenzformen religiöser Erhafrung*. Edited by Hubert Cancik. Düsseldorf: Patmos Verlag, 1978, pp. 59-77.

Schutz, Alfred. *Collected Papers II: Studies in Social Theory*. Edited by Arvid Brodersen. Phaenomenologica, Vol. 15. The Hague: Martinus Nijhoff, 1964.

Scott, Nathan A. Jr. *The Broken Center: Studies in the Theological Horizon of Modern Literature*. New Haven: Yale University Press, 1966.

Shulman, David Dean. *The King and the Clown in South Indian Myth and Poetry*. Princeton: Princeton University Press, 1985.

The Śiva Purāṇa. 4 Vols. Translated by a Board of Scholars. Delhi: Motilal Banarsidass, 1969-1970.

Spear, Percival. *A History of India*. Vol. II. Middlesex: Penguin Books, Ltd., 1965; reprint 1978.

Stephen, Alexander. *Hopi Journal*. Edited by Elsie Clews Parsons. Columbia University Contributions to Anthropology 25, vol. 1. 1936.

Syrkin, Alexander Y. "On the Behavior of the 'Fool for Christ's Sake'." *History of Religions* 22, no. 2 (November 1982): 150-171.

Titiev, Mischa. *The Hopi Indians of Old Oraibi: Change and Continuity*. Ann Arbor: University of Michigan Press, 1972.

Tracy, David. *The Analogical Imagination: Christian Theology and the Culture of Pluralism*. New York: Crossroads, 1981.

Trueblood, Elton. *The Humor of Christ*. New York: Harper and Row, Publishers, 1964.

Turner, Victor W. *The Ritual Process: Structure and Anti-Structure*. Chicago: Aldine Publishing Company, 1969.

Varenne, Jean. *Yoga and the Hindu Tradition*. Translated by Derek Coltman. Chicago and London: University of Chicago Press, 1976.

Vāyu Purāṇa. Bombay: Śrī-Venkaṭeśvara Steam Press, 1895.

Vecsey, Christopher. *Traditional Ojibwa Religion and Its Historical Changes*. Philadelphia: The American Philosophical Society, 1983.

Vivekananda, Swami. *The Complete Works of Swami Vivekananda*. Vol. 3. Tenth Edition. Calcutta: Advaita Ashrama, 1970.

Viṣṇu Purāṇa. Gorakhpur: Gita Press, n.d.

Walker, J. R. "The Sun Dance and other Ceremonies of the Oglala Division of the Teton Dakota." *Anthropology Papers of the American Museum* 16 (1917): 51- 223.

Wallace, Anthony F. C. *Religion: An Anthropological Viewpoint*. New York: Random House, 1966. .

________. "Revitalization Movements." *American Anthropologist* 58 (1956): 264-281.

Welbon, Guy R. and Yocum, Glenn E. eds. *Religious Festivals in South India and Sri Lanka*. New Delhi: Manohar Publications, 1982.

White, Charles S. J. "Kṛṣṇa as Divine Child." *History of Religions* 10, no. 2 (1970): 156-177.

Williams, George M. "The Ramakrishna Movement: A Study in Religious Change." In Robert D. Baird ed. *Religion in Modern India.* New Delhi: Manohar Publications, 1981, pp. 55-79. .

_______. "Svami Vivekananda: Archetypal Hero or Doubting Saint?." In Robert D. Baird ed. *Religion in Modern India.* New Delhi: Manohar Publications, 1981, pp. 197-226.

Wilson, Bryan. *Magic and the Millennium: A Sociological Study of Religious Movements of Protest Among Tribal and Third-World Peoples.* London: Heinemann, 1973.

Wissler, Clark. *Field Notes on the Dakota Indians, Collected on Museum Expedition of 1902.* New York: Museum of Natural History, 1904.

Woods, James Haughton, trans. *The Yoga-System of Patañjali.* Harvard Oriental Series Vol. 17. Cambridge: Harvard University Press, 1914; reprint New Delhi: Motilal Banarsidass, 1966.

Wulff, Donna Marie. "On Practicing Religiously: Music as Sacred in India." In Joyce Irwin ed. *Sacred Sound: Music in Religious Thouqht and Practice.* Thematic Studies 50/1. Chico, CA: Scholars Press, 1984, pp. 149-172.

Yocum, Glenn E. *Hymns to the Dancing Śiva: A Study of Māṇikkavācakar's Tiruvācakam.* Columbia, MO: South Asia Books, 1982. .

_______. "'Madness' and Devotion in Māṇikkavācakar's Tiruvācakam." In Fred W. Clothey and J. Bruce Long eds. *Experiencing Śiva: Encounters with a Hindu Deity.* New Delhi: Manohar, 1983, pp. 19-36.

Zimmer, Heinrich. "Die Indische Weltmutter." *Eranos Jahrbuch* 6 (1938): 175-220.

Zucker, Wolfgang M. "The Clown as the Lord of Disorder." *Theology Today* 24, 3 (October 1967): 306-317.

www.ingramcontent.com/pod-product-compliance
Ingram Content Group UK Ltd.
Pitfield, Milton Keynes, MK11 3LW, UK
UKHW041428180426
11947UKWH00007B/337

9 781555 403409